CYPRUS BC

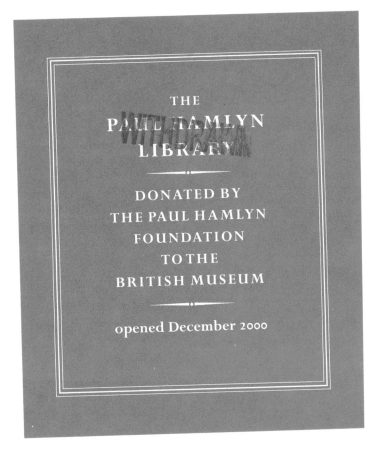

CYPRUS BC
7000 YEARS OF HISTORY

Edited by Veronica Tatton-Brown
with contributions by V. Karageorghis, E. J. Peltenburg, S. Swiny

Published for the Trustees of the British Museum by British Museum Publications Limited

© 1979, The Trustees of the British Museum
ISBN 0 7141 1265 8 *(cased)*
ISBN 0 7141 1266 6 *(paper)*
Published by British Museum Publications Ltd
6 Bedford Square, London WC1B 3RA

Designed by Gerald Cinamon
Printed in Great Britain by
W. S. Cowell Ltd, at the Butter Market, Ipswich

Acknowledgements

The idea for an exhibition of ancient Cypriote art in London was conceived about four years ago. Sir David Hunt, former British High Commissioner in Cyprus and the then Keeper and Deputy Keeper of the Department of Greek and Roman Antiquities, Mr D. E. L. Haynes and Dr R. A. Higgins, welcomed and promoted the idea which was accepted by the Trustees of the British Museum and the Cyprus Government. The actual organisation of the exhibition has fallen on the shoulders of the present Keeper of the Greek and Roman Department, Mr B. F. Cook, and Assistant Keeper, Dr V. A. Tatton-Brown, who have been helped at every stage by all their colleagues in the Department. They are most grateful to Dr M. R. Price, Deputy Keeper, Department of Coins and Medals, for arranging the display of coins in the ante-room. They received support too from the central services, in particular Miss Jean Rankine, Deputy Keeper, the members of the Design Office and the Public Relations Office. The enlarged photographs in the exhibition were prepared from negatives kindly provided by the Department of Antiquities of Cyprus, Dr E. J. Peltenburg (Lemba and Ayios Epiktetos) and Professor J. R. Carpenter (Phaneromeni), and by the Photographic Service of the British Museum which assisted also in other ways. In Cyprus all members of the staff of the Department of Antiquities offered their co-operation in every field. Let them all find here an expression of deep gratitude.

The editor of the catalogue would like to thank Dr V. Karageorghis, Dr E. J. Peltenburg and Mr S. Swiny not only for their contributions but also for their invaluable assistance over and above these. Academic help and advice has also been kindly given by Mr D. M. Bailey, Mr B. F. Cook, Dr D. B. Harden, Dr R. A. Higgins, Dr R. S. Merrillees and Mr T. W. T. Tatton-Brown. In the production a particular debt is owed to the editorial assistant, Miss Blanche Osborn, to Miss Susan Bird, who drew the maps and line illustrations, and to British Museum Publications Ltd.

VASSOS KARAGEORGHIS
Director, Department of Antiquities, Cyprus

Contents

Figures in *italic* indicate catalogue numbers

Introduction

The British public has long been familiar, in one way or another, with the art and archaeology of Cyprus. The British Museum, the Ashmolean Museum at Oxford and the Fitzwilliam Museum at Cambridge have been exhibiting ancient Cypriote artefacts since the end of the nineteenth century and the long association between Cyprus and Great Britain has given many British citizens the opportunity to visit the monuments and the museums in the island. This, however, does not mean that an exhibition of Cypriote antiquities in Great Britain is superfluous.

It was in the last century that Cyprus was put on the archaeological map. Travellers recorded their experiences, describing and identifying ancient sites and antiquities they discovered. Activity increased in the last twenty years before Cyprus was ceded to the British in 1878 and a number of foreign museums built up considerable collections from excavations conducted by amateurs. Among these early excavators the most famous was General Luigi Palma di Cesnola who was simultaneously American consul in Larnaca and Russian consul. The British restriction on unofficial excavations imposed in 1878 followed by the establishment of the Cyprus Museum in 1883 were the first steps towards setting Cypriote archaeology on a sound footing. At the end of 1878 a German, Max Ohnesfalsch-Richter, arrived in Cyprus and the first years of British rule were dominated by his excavations carried out with government authorisation.

Official British excavations began in 1889 under the auspices of the Cyprus Exploration Fund, set up by a body of scholars interested in Cypriote antiquities at the end of 1887. J. L. Myres, later Wykeham Professor of Ancient History at the University of Oxford, who may be described as one of the fathers of Cypriote archaeology, arrived in the island in 1894 and took part in the later British campaigns.

Between 1927 and 1931 the Swedish Cyprus Expedition conducted a series of scientific excavations on sites of different periods. In 1934 a government department responsible for archaeology, the Department of Antiquities, was established. J. Hilton was its first Director but after two years was succeeded by A. H. S. Megaw who held the post until the end of

British rule in 1960. The years after 1931 saw the investigation of a number of sites both by the Department of Antiquities of Cyprus and by foreign expeditions including teams from Britain, America, France and Australia. In 1955 the Department initiated a systematic archaeological survey of the island which recorded valuable evidence relating to the distribution of settlements.

In recent years, since 1960, the activity of the Department of Antiquities and of foreign expeditions has grown considerably. The first Cypriote Director of Antiquities, P. Dikaios, was succeeded by the present Director in 1963 and at the time Dr K. Nicolaou was appointed curator of the Museum, a post which he held until his retirement last autumn. During the last ten years or so Cypriote archaeology has achieved unprecedented popularity and Cypriote art is no longer considered as a dull provincial side-product of other neighbouring cultures. British scholarship contributed considerably towards this new development and a great number of young British scholars are now actively engaged in revealing the island's fascinating past.

Cyprus, situated between Europe and Asia, has over the centuries been a prey to warring factions seeking supremacy. The population, virtually from the beginning of the island's history, has been multifarious and the different communities since the rise of the city kingdoms in the first millennium BC have not always lived in peace with each other. The last three decades have seen considerable distress in the island; since the invasion of Cyprus by the Turkish army in 1974 rich museums like that at Famagusta and at Kyrenia (the latter houses the remains of a fine Greek ship sunk off the north coast at the end of the fourth century BC), and a number of important archaeological sites including Salamis, Enkomi and Soloi have been inaccessible to the staff of the Department of Antiquities.

Recent excavations in Cyprus, carried out by foreign and Cypriote archaeologists, have changed considerably our knowledge of Cypriote archaeology and added new chapters both to the island's cultural history and her artistic repertoire. Prehistory came into the limelight as a result of astonishing discoveries.

A whole range of Neolithic settlements, dating from the seventh to the fourth millennia BC have now been revealed, throwing new light on this remote period which constitutes the dawn of Cypriote history. Already at this early stage the art of Cyprus shows vivacity and originality, qualities which become even more apparent during subsequent periods. The culture of the Neolithic period had not been discovered when the British archaeologists explored Cyprus late in the nineteenth century and consequently there are few artefacts in the museums of Great Britain belonging to this period. It is interesting

however, that the first Neolithic object to be discovered in Cyprus, a stone bowl, found its way to Scotland in 1915, some twenty years before the 'official' discovery of the Neolithic settlement of Khirokitia!

The Chalcolithic period (literally 'copper-stone' age) is also a relatively recently discovered cultural phase in the archaeology of Cyprus, and Chalcolithic art is practically unknown in the museums of the United Kingdom. Its fine and imaginative artistic production is unique among prehistoric cultures in the Mediterranean region and heralds the exuberance

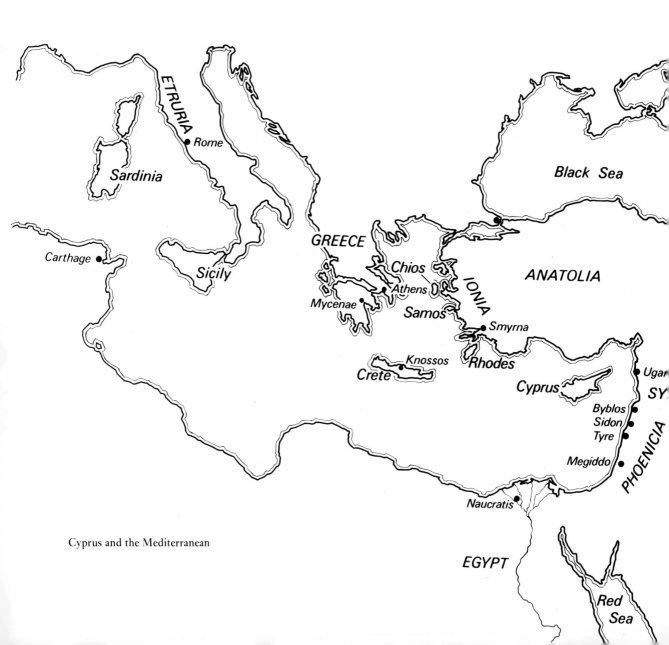

Cyprus and the Mediterranean

and originality which characterize Cypriote art throughout its history. Current excavations carried out by British scholars at Lemba have revealed impressive architectural monuments and artistic documents which justify the special place which this period occupies in this exhibition.

The Bronze Age, particularly the Late Bronze Age, has a special significance for Cyprus, which is well known for her copper mines. Excavations at Enkomi, Kition, Hala Sultan Tekké, Palaepaphos and elsewhere have brought to light monumental architecture and revealed new aspects of the art, religion,

political and social structure of Cyprus during those formative years of the second half of the second millennium BC. It is true that the wealth and artistic production of Late Bronze Age Cyprus became well known after the excavations of tombs at Enkomi carried out under the auspices of the British Museum. As a result fine jewellery, ivory, bronzes and Mycenaean vases in the pictorial style have been among the prize exhibits of the British Museum for nearly a century. However, it was only recently that large portions of towns of this period revealed their secrets.

The Iron Age was an adventurous period for Cyprus, which found itself an easy prey to the antagonism of the great empires of the Near East. The artistic production reflects the political adventures. Based on their Bronze Age culture the Cypriots adopted cultural influences from the Near East which they adapted to their own taste, thus creating a truly Cypriote art, which is at the same time both conservative and lively. Themes and motives of Near Eastern art, brought in by the Phoenicians from the ninth century BC onwards, enriched the repertory of Cypriote craftsmen. Cypriote vase painting of the pictorial style of the eighth and seventh centuries BC is a characteristic product of this new era. Lively and colourful compositions rendered with a developed sense of humour illustrate one of the highlights of Cypriote artistic production. Though the museums of Great Britain, particularly the British Museum, possess a good number of vases of this style, yet it is only during recent years that they have become widely known and appreciated.

Recent excavations at Kition have brought to light new evidence of the extent and importance of the Phoenician presence in Cyprus. The great temple of Astarte is one of the largest of its kind in the Mediterranean and could perhaps be compared with the equally impressive temple of Aphrodite at Palaepaphos. Both, however, had Late Bronze Age antecedents, as excavations have now shown. Silver bowls, bronzes and ivories, bear witness to the contribution of this Levantine people in the development of the art of Cyprus and also of what is known as Orientalizing art in Greece. Cyprus must have played an important role in these cultural exchanges between the orient and the occident.

The excavations of the Department of Antiquities in the necropolis of Salamis (1962–73) have opened

a new phase in Cypriote archaeology and even in Mediterranean archaeology in general. Impressive 'royal' tombs, their chambers and facades built of fine stone blocks and furnished with rich gifts, reflect the wealth of the capital of Cyprus and the power of the Salaminian kings. A large quantity of Greek pottery of the Late Geometric style (eighth century BC) was found in one of them. This has been ingeniously interpreted as the dowry of a Greek princess married to one of the Salaminian kings which, if correct, would emphasise and confirm renewed contacts between Cyprus and Greece in the eighth century at the time when the Greeks were beginning their colonial expansion in the Near East. The horse and chariot burials found in the *dromoi* (entrance passages) of the 'royal' tombs of Salamis illustrate very eloquently 'homeric' burial customs which are now being found in other lands of the Mediterranean, and even as far as the Atlantic coast of Spain. Ivory chairs and thrones, bronze cauldrons and gilded horse trappings found in the *dromoi* of the Salaminian tombs, illustrate some of the objects which Homer knew and admired from the world of the Phoenicians.

The excavations of the city site of Salamis from 1952 until 1974 were expected to reveal some of the wealth and splendour of the palaces and other public buildings of the Archaic and Classical periods. They uncovered part of the Roman town and some Hellenistic remains but were abruptly brought to an end in the summer of 1974. The Gymnasium with the impressive colonnade of its Palaestra and the well preserved Baths, the large Theatre and the Early Christian basilicas illustrate the glory of this city which was the capital of Cyprus for about one thousand years. It should be mentioned that the site attracted British archaeologists as early as 1890 and as a result of their excavations the museums of Great Britain acquired some fine marble statues of the Roman period, but it was only with the researches of 1952–73 that the monumental public buildings of the northern sector of Salamis were completely uncovered and correctly identified. The rich harvest of marble statues from the Gymnasium and the Theatre enriched considerably the collections of the Cyprus Museum.

New excavations started during recent years in the main city states of Cyprus, which were inde-

Map of Cyprus

Ancient place names are italicised where they coincide with a modern village

pendent kingdoms throughout the Archaic and Classical periods. Amathus, Tamassos, Paphos and Kourion have come to the foreground of archaeological activity once more and promise to produce important archaeological monuments. Tombs with stone built chambers and façades and Hellenistic public buildings at Amathus; late Archaic to Classical remains of a sanctuary at Tamassos; Hellenistic and

Roman remains at Nea Paphos, and Roman remains at Kourion, are a few of the recent discoveries which have been made, not to mention an impressive number of monumental Early Christian basilicas at Salamis, Amathus, Nea Paphos, Kourin and elsewhere. The most popular of the new discoveries, however, are the two palatial villas of the Roman period at Nea Paphos, with their spacious rooms and porticos, the floors of which are decorated with polychrome mosaics depicting mythological scenes. Nea Paphos was in fact the capital of Cyprus during the Roman period. Kourion has also produced important mosaic floors in an area of the Acropolis, where a number of public buildings are now being excavated. At the temple and precinct of Apollo, outside the walls of the same town, a new era of excavations has recently been inaugurated, in order to reveal completely the remains of this important sacred area where Apollo was worshipped from the eighth century BC down to the end of the Roman period.

Soloi was also the scene of great archaeological activity from 1965 to 1974. A Hellenistic Palace, a Roman Agora, a Roman Nymphaeum and a spacious Early Christian basilica are but a few of the monuments which the archaeological spade started to reveal.

The above is a very short survey, far from being exhaustive, of the main archaeological discoveries in Cyprus during recent years. Fifteen or more foreign archaeological missions from many countries of the world, working side by side with the archaeologists of the Cyprus Department of Antiquities, have brought Cypriote archaeology to the foreground of archaeological research and have given Cyprus a prominent place on the archaeological map of the Mediterranean. The fruits of these recent researches are now available for international scholarship through the numerous publications of the results of the excavations. This new impetus in the study of Cypriote archaeology created a popular interest in the island's cultural heritage and it is with this in mind that the Department of Antiquities

decided to make the treasures of ancient Cypriote art, which are kept in the Cyprus Museum in Nicosia, known to a wide international public. The exhibition of the 'Treasures of Cyprus', which has toured many centres of Europe and America during the last ten years, aroused a lively interest among the public in an art which was so original and so lively and which they encountered often for the first time.

The exhibition which has been sent to the United Kingdom (London and Birmingham) is quite unique of its kind and differs completely from all others hitherto sent outside Cyprus. It is confined to the pre-Christian periods and is composed of the best specimens which the museums of Cyprus possess. They include masterpieces which leave Cyprus for the first time, in an effort to show to the British public a complete picture of our artistic heritage, bearing in mind the demands of the British public and the fact that London is one of the most important centres of world cultural activities. May the message of culture sent by this exhibition help to bring reason to humanity and free the nations of the world from the folly of war and destruction.

VASSOS KARAGEORGHIS

Chronological Table

(The absolute dates are approximate)

Neolithic, Khirokitia culture		7000–6000 BC
Neolithic, Sotira culture		4500–3750 BC
Chalcolithic	I	3500–2500/2300 BC
Early Bronze Age	I	2300–2075 BC
	II	2075–2000 BC
	III	2000–1900 BC
Middle Bronze Age	I	1900–1800 BC
	II	1800–1725 BC
	III	1725–1625 BC
Late Bronze Age	I	1625–1450 BC
	II	1450–1225 BC
	III	1225–1050 BC
Geometric	I	1050–950 BC
	II	950–850 BC
	III	850–750 BC
Archaic	I	750–600 BC
	II	600–475 BC
Classical	I	475–400 BC
	II	400–325 BC

Note: The date and terminology for the Neolithic and Chalcolithic periods follow the scheme proposed by E. J. Peltenburg, *Levant* X (1978) 55 ff. The Bronze Age dates are based on those suggested by R. S. Merrillees, *RDAC* (1977) 33ff. In the Iron Age (Geometric to Classical) for the most part we have adopted Gjerstad's chronology outlined in *SCE* IV.2 except that we have raised the date of the beginning of the Archaic period to 750 BC which agrees with the findings of recent research.

Notes on the Catalogue

ABBREVIATIONS

Authors

V.K.	V. Karageorghis
E.J.P.	E. J. Peltenburg
S.S.	S. Swiny
V.A.T-B.	V. A. Tatton-Brown

Measurements

all dimensions are in centimetres

L: length
W: width
H: height
D: diameter
Th: thickness

Departments

Cyprus Archaeological Survey: The archaeological survey unit in Cyprus.
Department of Antiquities: Department of Antiquities in Cyprus.
GR: Department of Greek and Roman Antiquities, British Museum.

PLACE NAMES

The spelling is that in common usage.

When objects come from a particular area of a site, the exact location follows the site name, e.g. Palaepaphos, Evreti.

ARRANGEMENT

The objects are arranged as far as possible in chronological order. At certain periods particular sites are singled out and the finds for the most part displayed together (e.g. Enkomi and Kition in the Late Bronze Age). The chronological sequence is not strictly followed when this would disrupt the story (e.g. finds from eighth-century Salamis and Kition belonging to the Geometric period are alongside the Archaic material from those sites).

*Unfortunately it has not been possible to include catalogue numbers 6, 218, and 341–343 in the exhibition; these items are marked with an asterisk in the text.

The Neolithic Period

Our record of human occupation in Cyprus starts belatedly in the Neolithic period about 7000 BC. Cypriote civilization was to continue as it began by contrasting sharply with that of its neighbours in the eastern Mediterranean.

The first inhabitants, who perhaps came from the nearby Syrian coast visible to the east, were thinly spread. They lived in small villages consisting of distinctive circular brick and stone buildings *(tholoi)* on sites chosen for their defensible locations. The dead were buried under the floors of these buildings, in particular at the unusually large settlement at Khirokitia where the skeletons occasionally wear necklaces (as nos. 4–6). There is also evidence for the artificial deformation of skulls from childhood. The settlers either arrived with or traded for Anatolian obsidian (a volcanic glass) and Levantine carnelian; they kept sheep and goats and grew barley, which they harvested with fine sickle blades. However, in spite of the work involved to provide the staple ingredients for living, there was still time for stylised art forms in hard stone and clay to be developed (nos. 2, 3, 7). This Khirokitia culture flickered briefly only to be eclipsed or altogether extinguished in a prehistoric 'Dark Age' lasting some 1500 years from about 6000 to about 4500 BC during which there are only tenuous hints of any population on the island.

Communities of the Sotira culture, named after an extensively explored site near the south coast, have no connections with the earliest island inhabitants other than the occasional preference for the same situations. Their settlements consisted of stone-based, single-roomed houses with circular platform hearths and benches against the walls. They buried their dead outside the houses in small pits. The pottery of the north with boldly painted designs is distinguished from that of the south which bears intricate combed decoration but the bowls and jugs of both regions are similar. Otherwise the sites of the period (about twenty-five have now been recognised) were remarkably uniform. They were relatively short-lived agricultural villages whose surviving artefacts show that they were in contact with each other but isolated from the adjacent mainland. In addition to the foodstuffs known previously in the Khirokitia culture, grapes and olives, characteristic Mediterranean products, were now gathered; remains of fallow deer are so common at some sites that it seems that they were at times herded.

In this period there are no buildings or monuments which stand out as particularly important and it is therefore difficult to ascertain whether the society had a hierarchy. Nonetheless the inhabitants during the Sotira culture made the most of their insular environment. Villages grew in size and most regions of the island were now occupied, apart from the central plain, the mountains and the west. The origins of the culture are obscure and its demise apparently rapid; many locations were abandoned and in one case the excavator believed that he found evidence for an earthquake. However, enough links with the succeeding period exist to demonstrate that the Sotira culture sees the beginning of many specifically Cypriote traditions. [E. J. P.]

1 Stone bowl, dark grey andesite
Neolithic (7000–6000 BC)
Khirokitia, Tholos XVII; Department of Antiquities excavations.
Shallow, rectangular spouted bowl. Geometric decoration in relief on the outside. Repaired in antiquity. L 30·5; W 16·5–27·5; H 10.
Bibliography: Dikaios (1953), 109, no. 813, fig. 52, pls 56, 122; Buchholz and Karageorghis (1973), 156, no. 1657.
Cyprus Museum, Nicosia.

2 Conical stone, andesite
Neolithic (7000–6000 BC)
Khirokitia; Department of Antiquities excavations.
Engraved decoration forming a latticed pattern. H 5·8; D 6.
Several conical stones were found on this site. Their purpose is unknown but, like the idols, they may well have had a religious significance.
Bibliography: Dikaios (1953), 342, no. 12, pls 89, 138; Buchholz and Karageorghis (1973), 155, no. 1662.
Cyprus Museum, Nicosia.

3 Head of unfired clay
Neolithic (7000–6000 BC)
Khirokitia, Tholos XLVII; Department of Antiquities excavations.
Eyes, nose and mouth indicated. Wavy lines in relief on the back of the head depict the hair or perhaps snakes. H 10·5.

3

4

Snakes as symbols of the cthonic or underworld deities are seen on the Vounous sanctuary models (nos. 54, 55). If these wavy lines are indeed snakes the religious significance of the early idols would be confirmed.

Bibliography: Dikaios (1953), 183, no. 1063, pls. 98, 144; Buchholz and Karageorghis (1973), 160, no. 1698.

Cyprus Museum, Nicosia.

4 Stone and shell necklace

Neolithic (7000–6000 B C)
Khirokitia, Tholos XVII; Department of Antiquities excavations.
Composed of eighteen dentalium shells and twenty-one carnelian beads. L 52·6.

Bibliography: Dikaios (1953), 109, no. 560, fig. 52, pl. 99; Buchholz and Karageorghis (1973), 166, no. 1769.

Cyprus Museum, Nicosia.

5 Stone and shell necklace

Neolithic (7000–6000 B C)
Khirokitia, Tholos XIX; Department of Antiquities excavations.

Composed of groups of three or four dentalium shells alternating with carnelian beads. A flat piece of picrolite acts as a link in the middle. L 40.

Bibliography: Dikaios (1953), 118, no. 1485, fig. 58, pl. 68A; Buchholz and Karageorghis (1973), 166, no. 1767.

Cyprus Museum, Nicosia.

*6 Stone and shell necklace

Neolithic (7000–6000 B C)
Khirokitia, Tholos XVIII; Department of Antiquities excavations.

Composed of dentalium shells and six carnelian beads. L 35.

Bibliography: Dikaios (1953), 112, no. 928a, fig. 54; Buchholz and Karageorghis (1973), 166, no. 1768.

Cyprus Museum, Nicosia.

7 Stone idol, andesite

Neolithic (7000–6000 B C)
Khirokitia; Department of Antiquities excavations.
Flat body and round head with facial features crudely indicated and scoring on the back to show the hair. Legs divided by vertical grooves. No arms. Probably unfinished. H 19.

Bibliography: Dikaios (1953), 391, no. 967, pls. 95, 143; Buchholz and Karageorghis (1973), 160, no. 1693.

Cyprus Museum, Nicosia.

8

8 Spouted bowl, combed ware
Neolithic (4500–3750 BC)
Khirokitia; Department of Antiquities excavations.
Decorated with wavy lines. H 15; D 32·5.

Bibliography: Dikaios (1953), 361f., no. 496, pls. 71, 135; Buchholz and Karageorghis (1973), 144, no. 1487.

Cyprus Museum, Nicosia.

The Chalcolithic Period

The term Chalcolithic (literally copper-stone) is used in Cypriote archaeology to denote the period when metal first appeared but was still uncommon. Radiocarbon dates (obtained by scientific analysis of organic materials), for this, as for previous periods, suggest a longer duration than was formerly supposed and reveal times when evidence is lacking, in particular some five hundred years between the Neolithic and fully-fledged Chalcolithic. Chalcolithic settlements have been excavated mainly in the vicinity of Erimi near Sotira and Lemba near Paphos. The western end of the island now seems to have been inhabited for the first time and this expansion of occupied territory coincides with a considerable increase in the number of villages compared with those of the late Neolithic period.

Certain typical pottery traditions of the previous age linger into this and so, despite many cultural innovations, it seems unlikely that the population was entirely new. After a modest start the Erimi culture at its height extended over most of the island. People now lived in circular buildings with conical roofs and some were clearly reserved for various special functions. There are three other important new features in this period: the increasing use of metal, changes in burial customs, and a new type of miniature sculpture. The advent of metal tolled the death knell for traditional stone industries. Utilitarian objects like chisels and hooks as well as jewellery (no. 40) were now hammered into shape from copper. This is a breakthrough of the first importance since, whether the metal was locally mined or imported, its manufacture into different items probably involved foreign contact; Cyprus henceforth increasingly takes part in international commerce. Burial customs became more elaborate; at Souskiou in the newly settled western area there are cemeteries richly furnished with grave goods. Both the practice of burying the dead in cemeteries and supplying grave goods are new developments which foreshadow Bronze Age customs. Perhaps the most unexpected innovation, however, is the appearance of a new kind of figurine, the canonical type shaped as a taut cruciform and usually made of steatite (nos. 10–18, 23–25); clay examples are more diverse in shape (nos. 29–31). Resemblances to figurines from elsewhere are slight; the imaginative vitality and the independence of this creative activity, the uniformity of theme and the concentration in the west are the most striking elements of the achievement.

Towards the end of the period, several poorly understood but evidently momentous changes took place in the north. Metalwork, ornaments, burial customs and pottery alter, the last showing affinity with Anatolian wares. Since Cyprus had contacts with Anatolia where there is evidence for dramatic upheavals, it is unlikely that the changes on the island can be viewed in isolation. It remains to be seen to what extent newcomers were responsible for ushering in the Bronze Age, but it is at least clear that while the changes were profound, they did not occur everywhere at the same time as the late Erimi culture persisted longer in the south and west.   [E. J. P.]

9 Stone idol, andesite
Chalcolithic (3500–2500 BC)
Ayia Mavri, near Salamiou.
Round head with depressions for facial features and hair shown by grooves; stumpy arms and legs. w 10·3; H 16.
Bibliography: Buchholz and Karageorghis (1973), 160, no. 1689.
Paphos Museum. 1503.

10 Steatite cruciform idol, light green
Chalcolithic (3500–2500 BC)
Probably near Souskiou; purchased.
Almost triangular body, no legs and no facial features indicated. w 3·7; H 6·5.
Bibliography: Karageorghis, *BCH* CI (1977), 713 f., fig. 8a.
Cyprus Museum, Nicosia. 1976/VIII–10/1.

11 Steatite cruciform idol, light green
Chalcolithic (3500–2500 BC)
Probably from near Souskiou; purchased.
As no. 10. w 5·4; H 6·5.
Bibliography: Karageorghis, *BCH* CI (1977), 713 f., fig. 8b.
Cyprus Museum, Nicosia. 1976/VIII–10/2.

12 Steatite cruciform idol
Chalcolithic (3500–2500 BC)
Unknown provenance.

Facial features shown in relief. Hatching across the arms and on the back of the head to show the hair. Deep groove divides the legs and forms pubic triangle. H 13·5.
Bibliography: Buchholz and Karageorghis (1973), 160, no. 1701; Vagnetti, *RDAC* (1974), 30, pl. 5·2.
Cyprus Museum, Nicosia. W 290.

13

13 Steatite cruciform idol
Chalcolithic (3500–2500 BC)
Yialia.
Stylised figure wearing a necklace with cruciform pendant shown in relief. Hair, eyes and nose also in relief. Legs separated by a deep groove. H 15·3.
Bibliography: Dikaios. *RDAC* (1934), 16, no. 10, pl. 16·1; Buchholz and Karageorghis (1973), 160, no. 1699; Vagnetti, *RDAC* (1974), 28, pl. 5·1.
Cyprus Museum, Nicosia. 1934/III–2/2.

14 Steatite cruciform double idol
Chalcolithic (3500–2500 BC)
Salamiou, Anephani.

14

Male and female joined together at right angles so that each uses the other's body as arms. Facial features shown in relief. Deep groove divides legs and outline of body, also marking the feet. Modelled breasts. W 8·8; H 9·3.

    Bibliography: Buchholz and Karageorghis (1973), 160, no. 1700.

    Cyprus Museum, Nicosia. 1959/XI–3/6.

15 Steatite cruciform pendant

Chalcolithic (3500–2500 BC)

Palaepaphos, Vathyrkakas, Tomb 1; Swiss-German excavations.

Suspension hole in the top of the head. Deep groove separates legs. Hands and feet indicated by incisions. H 3.

    Bibliography: Karageorghis, *BCH* XCVII (1973), 681, fig. 115; Vagnetti, *RDAC* (1974), 24.

    Cyprus Museum, Nicosia. Vathyrkakas T 1/1.

16 Steatite cruciform pendant

Chalcolithic (3500–2500 BC)

Palaepaphos, Vathyrkarkas, Tomb 1; Swiss-German excavations.

Suspension hole through the centre of face. Body narrows into a triangle to form schematic legs. Legs broken. H 2.

Bibliography: Karageorghis, *BCH* XCVII (1973), 681.
Cyprus Museum, Nicosia. Vathyrkakas T 1/2.

17 Three steatite cruciform pendants

Chalcolithic (3500–2500 BC)

Palaepaphos, Vathyrkakas, Tomb 7; Swiss-German excavations.

Suspension hole through the centre of the face. The body narrows into a triangle to form schematic legs. H 1·5–2.

    Bibliography: Karageorghis, *BCH* XCVII (1973) 681.

    Cyprus Museum, Nicosia. Vathyrkakas T 7/1–3.

18 Two steatite cruciform pendants

Chalcolithic (3500–2500 BC)

Palaepaphos, Vathyrkakas, Tomb 17; Swiss-German excavations.

Each has an elongated neck and suspension hole through the centre of the face. The body narrows into a triangle to form schematic legs. H 3 and 3·5.

    Bibliography: Karageorghis, *BCH* XCVII (1973), 681.

    Cyprus Museum, Nicosia. Vathyrkakas T 17/1–2.

19 Stone and shell necklace

Chalcolithic (3500–2500 BC)

Palaepaphos, Varkyrkakas, Tomb 3; Department of Antiquities excavations.

19

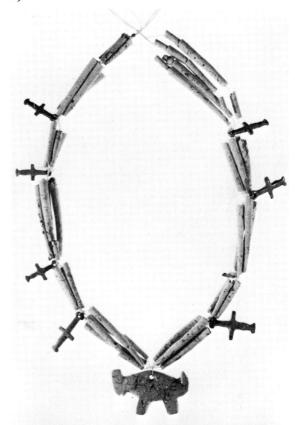

Composed of groups of dentalium shells alternating with steatite pendants. Eight of these are cruciform idols (one now missing) and the ninth, in the centre, is a quadruped. One cruciform pendant missing. L 35; H 2.

Bibliography: Karageorghis, *BCH* XCVII (1973), 637, fig. 69; Vagnetti, *RDAC* (1974), 28.

Cyprus Museum, Nicosia.

20 Deep bowl, Red-on-White ware
Chalcolithic (3500–2500 BC)
Palaepaphos, Vathyrkakas, Tomb 3; Department of Antiquities excavations.
Decorated with triangles of red dots. H 11·1; D 11·2.

Bibliography: Karageorghis, *BCH* XCVII (1973), 637, fig. 68.

Kouklia Museum.

Lemba Chalcolithic Settlement

Although only one of several Chalcolithic sites in western Cyprus, Lemba is important since it is the first of these earliest metal-using communities of Cyprus to be investigated extensively. Three areas have been excavated in three short seasons.

The earliest trace of human activity comes from Kissonerga Mosphilia which may have been a founder colony. It was to become the largest Chalcolithic settlement at Lemba and has produced the finest artefacts. Deep hollows were discovered in the terraces at Kissonerge Mylouthkia but no proper floor surfaces. The finds included red burnished platters or bowls, at present unique.

Lemba Lakkous comprises some seven acres beside a stream near the coast. The site was occupied intermittently by people who perhaps at first spent much of their time out-of-doors; they constructed shelters for storage jars and the like, and subsequently built low circular huts, set irregularly on slight terraces. These buildings, which were destroyed about 2500 BC, served as kitchens, workshops and other specialised units rather than consistently as houses. Pit graves, mainly for children who were laid on their right sides in a flexed position, were dug within the walls and under the floors. Sometimes communication holes were provided between the graves and houses.

Cereal crops were cultivated and there is evidence that sheep, goats, pigs and deer were numerous. Some of the pottery and metal types show outside influences, probably the result of foreign trade. [E. J. P.]

21 Limestone female figurine
Chalcolithic (3000–2500 BC)
Lemba Lakkous Building 1; British excavations.
Fiddle-shaped female with outstretched arms, elongated neck, elliptical head with incised hair line and relief eyes and nose. Incised ⇓s on the body, the upper indicating breasts, the lower the pubic area. H 36.

Discovered in the debris of a destroyed building this unique figure shows that small sculpture did exist in Chalcolithic Cyprus, as well as pendant figures. It also suggests that the western part of the isle, normally regarded as a cultural backwater, was pre-eminent. In shape it conforms to the standard cruciform figure type except for the hips or legs which here form bulges, so balancing the arms and contrasting with the fine incisions.

21

Normally the pubic areas on steatite figures are not so accentuated. This is, however, a feature of clay figurines and such an innovation in steatite may be the result of a mixture of artistic conventions later in the period.
Bibliography: Karageorghis, *BCH* CI (1977), 744, fig. 66 left.
Cyprus Museum, Nicosia. LL 93.

24 Steatite female figurine, mottled green-brown
Chalcolithic (about 2500 BC)
Lemba Lakkous; British excavations.
Lower body. Broken at legs and arms, the latter polished for re-use. Incisions at front and back of legs, across hips for pubic triangle and in centre and along sides of torso. Possibly incised on two different occasions. W 3; H 5·2; Th 1·6.
Bibliography: Karageorghis, *BCH* CI (1977), 744, fig. 66 right.
Paphos Museum. LL 152.

25 Steatite cruciform female figurine, mottled green
Chalcolithic (about 2500 BC)
Lemba Lakkous, Building 2, grave 20; British excavations.
Projecting arms, small breasts and legs bent at the knees. Tilted square face with incised and relief details. Flat back. H 6·1.
This classic example of the cruciform type shows little sign of wear and so was presumably made especially for deposit in the grave. It is not yet certain whether the different styles denote different functions.
Bibliography: Karageorghis, *BCH* CII (1978), 911.
Cyprus Museum, Nicosia. LL 300.

Bibliography: Peltenburg, *Antiquity* LI (1977), 140ff.
Cyprus Museum, Nicosia. LL 54.

22 Limestone female figurine
Chalcolithic (3000–2500 BC)
Lemba, Kissonerga Mosphilia; British excavations.
Torso with plain, flat back, leg stumps severed from hips with simple Y incision. Depression in chest between broken arms. L 9·7; W 7·5; Th 3·9.
Limestone figurines are scarce in Chalcolithic Cyprus but this example shows that the Cypriots were capable of modelling in many media. The legs are either truncated or not depicted, as are those of examples from Erimi on the south coast.
Bibliography: Peltenburg, *Levant* XI (1979) fig. 8 (forthcoming).
Paphos Museum. KM 33.

23 Steatite female figurine, blue-green
Chalcolithic (3000–2500 BC)
Lemba Lakkous; British excavations.
Hips only with incised V for pubic area and characteristic bustle at the back. Fragmentary. H 7.

26 Steatite pendant, dark green-black mottled stone
Chalcolithic (about 2500 BC)
Lemba, Lakkous, Building 2; British excavations.
Thin plaque, trapezoidal, and pierced near the centre of one edge. L 2·7; W 3; Th 0·2.
Paphos Museum. LL 217.

27 Steatite pendant, green
Chalcolithic (3000–2500 BC)
Lemba, Lakkous; British excavations.
Sheared, with three globular segments. L 2·8; W 1·1; Th 0·8.
Paphos Museum. LL 241.

28 Steatite pendant, light green veined stone
Chalcolithic (3000–2500 BC)
Lemba, Kissonerga Mosphilia; British excavations.
Lotus pod with facetted body. L 3·1; W 1·7; Th 0·6.
Stylised fruit pendants are new in the Chalcolithic period. Their development may well be the result of foreign contacts.

Bibliography: Peltenburg, *Levant* XI (1979), fig. 8 (forthcoming).
Paphos Museum. KM 34.

29 Terracotta female figurine
Chalcolithic (about 2500–2200 BC)
Lemba, Kissonerga Mylouthkia; British excavations.
Cigar-shaped, with incisions for legs and between stumps of breasts. Arms and neck broken. L 10; W 3·3 Th 2·1.

This simple type of figurine was first discovered at Lemba. Its date shows that it belongs to an early stage in the evolution of the cruciform type and so is critical to our understanding of the whole style.
Paphos Museum. K. Myl. 58.

30 Painted terracotta leg of figurine, Red-on-White ware
Chalcolithic (about 2500–2200 BC)
Lemba, Kissonerga Mylouthkia; British excavations.
The broken foot is dull red, and the leg has two rows of strokes bordered by horizontal bands. Incomplete. L 8·5; D 2·9.
Paphos Museum. K. Myl. 85.

31 Painted terracotta leg of figurine, Red-on-White ware
Chalcolithic (3000–2500 BC)
Lemba, Kissonerga Mosphilia; British excavations.
Short foot with incised toes. Rows of irregularly latticed squares and other motifs above a row of vertical strokes are perhaps the fringe of a garment. L 9·3; D 4·7.

The size of this leg shows that large-scale terracotta figurines were also made like the limestone examples (e.g. no. 21). The painted decoration fades on the interior of this, the right leg, so it is not certain whether fringed trousers, or indeed any garment, are worn.
Bibliography: Karageorghis, *BCH* CII (1978), 911, fig. 73.
Paphos Museum. KM 61.

32 Incised terracotta disc
Chalcolithic (3000–2000 BC)
Lemba Lakkous; British excavations.
Slightly concave disc made from a vessel fragment, its exterior radially incised with two sets of irregular lines divided by an uneven circular line. About half remains. D 5·2; Th 5.

The markings on this disc are unique. They are too purposeful to be doodlings and too irregular to be decoration. Their significance is, however, as yet unknown.
Paphos Museum. LL 325.

33 Flask, Red-on-White ware
Chalcolithic (30000–2500 BC)
Lemba Lakkous, Building 1; British excavations.

33

Globular with pointed base, straight neck and everted rim. Red bands at mouth, shoulder and lower body on a white ground, lightly coated with dilute red paint. Nearly complete. D (mouth) 5·5, (body) 13·5; H 25·6.

This is a characteristic shape known in all the Chalcolithic settlements in Cyprus. It comes from the same building as no. 21.
Bibliography: Peltenburg, *Levant* XI (1979), fig. 10·10 (forthcoming).
Paphos Museum. LL 167.

34 Bowl, Red and Black Burnished ware
Chalcolithic (about 2500 BC)
Lemba Lakkous, Building 3; British excavations.
Deep bowl with straight, flaring sides. Unevenly fired, so that it becomes red and black. H 10; D 19.

Unpainted pottery, whose colour depends on the firing conditions, appears in Cyprus just before the beginning of the Bronze Age. Since painted pottery was favoured earlier, this plain ware is an important link between the two eras.
Bibliography: Peltenburg, *Levant* XI (1979), fig. 10·4 (forthcoming).
Paphos Museum. LL 378.

35 Bowl, Glossy Burnished ware
Chalcolithic (2500–2300 BC)
Lemba, Kissonerga Mylouthkia; British excavations.
Partly restored. H 9; D 22.
  Bibliography: Peltenburg, *Levant* XI (1979), fig. 10·3
(forthcoming).
  Paphos Museum. K. Myl. 87.

36 Rim of bowl, combed ware
Chalcolithic (3000–2750 BC)
Lemba, Kissonerga Mosphilia; British excavations.
Decorated with horizontal wavy bands on the inside and
diagonal wavy bands on the outside. Fragment. H 9; D 22.
  This vessel is particularly significant since it shows how
the combed decoration of the Neolithic period persisted
into the third millennium in western Cyprus which was
now inhabited for the first time. It therefore helps to pin-
point both the origin and the date of the earliest colonists in
this area.
  Bibliography: Peltenburg, *Levant* XI (1979), (forthcoming).
  Paphos Museum. KM 96.

37 Limestone conical seal
Chalcolithic (about 2500 BC)
Lemba Lakkous, Building 3; British excavations.
On the base an incised dotted circle and a spiral interrupted
at one side by radial lines. L 3·1; D 2·6.
  If this is indeed a seal used to stamp property or other
items it is about a thousand years earlier than any other

38

seals as yet found in Cyprus. Possibly those of the inter-
vening years were made of some perishable material such as
wood. Otherwise the use of seals at this period must have
been an isolated short-lived practice.
  Bibliography: Peltenburg, *Levant* XI (1979), fig. 9 left
(forthcoming).
  Paphos Museum. LL 211.

38 Stone adze
Chalcolithic (about 2500 BC)
Lemba Lakkous; British excavations.
Flat adze with straight, facetted sides evidently copying a
metal type. L 13·1; W 7·0; Th 1·5.
  Bibliography: Aikman, *RDAC* (1978), 26, pl. 3·4 left.
  Paphos Museum. LL 131.

39 Stone pestle, andesite
Chalcolithic (about 2500 BC)
Lemba Lakkous, Building 3; British excavations.
Bottle-shaped. L 24·5; D 4·8–9·5.
  Paphos Museum. LL 183.

37

39

40

40 Copper chisel
Chalcolithic (about 2500 BC)
Lemba Lakkous; British excavations.
Almost pure copper. Square in section, unevenly tapered.
L 9·1; W 0·6; TH 0·5.

This is one of the earliest copper tools from Cyprus, but whether it was manufactured locally or imported has not yet been established.

Bibliography: Karageorghis, *BCH* CI (1977), 744, fig.67.
Paphos Museum. LL 134.

The Early Bronze Age

The initial phase of the Early Bronze Age in Cyprus—commonly known as Chalcolithic III—shows an unbroken development from the earlier cultures, with an infusion of new and foreign ideas. Paramount amongst these is the knowledge of metal-working, for example the daggers from Vasilia (nos. 47–49), while the west Anatolian strain in some pottery shapes indicates the source of these new traits.

Our understanding of the Cypriote Early Bronze Age is distorted by the nature of the evidence. Hundreds of burials have been excavated—at Vounous and Lapithos especially—but not a single occupation site, and in the absence of written records our understanding of the period is primarily deduced from the funerary offerings.

From the modest beginnings in the river valleys of the western Mesaoria (e.g. Philia, Vasiliko) Early Bronze Age settlements spread widely throughout Cyprus, with the exception of the heavily wooded central plain and possibly the Paphos district. Water and agricultural land determined the choice of site, while access to the sea or copper ore deposits surrounding the Troodos massif, was evidently of comparatively minor importance.

A thriving economy supplemented by an emerging metallurgical industry led to better provision for the dead. They were buried in rock-cut chambers approached by an open passage known as a *dromos*, and the cave-like chamber was sealed by a large stone slab. In common with most of the ancient world the Cypriots believed in an after-life, and even humble burials were equipped with pottery vessels containing food, drink and unguents. The more fortunate might receive, in addition, utensils, tools and weapons.

The long sequence of Red Polished pottery which spans the Early and Middle Bronze Age is remarkable for its variety and power of expression. The exuberant shapes and decoration—both modelled and incised—are quite impracticable for domestic purposes, and were specifically intended for use as grave-goods. Towards the end of the period, terracotta models provide some insight into the life-style and religious beliefs (e.g. nos. 53–55).

How and where copper ores were first mined and smelted remains unknown, but the sheer quantity of tools and weapons made from copper and bronze, in a typically Cypriote style, bears witness to the smith's activity. A small number of imports reached Cyprus, possibly in return for copper, thereby drawing the island out of its previous isolation. [s. s.]

41 Bottle, Red Polished ware
Early Bronze Age (2300–2075 BC)
Philia, Vasiliko, Tomb 1; Department of Antiquities excavations.
Ovoid body, long neck, open spout at rim. Horn-like projection below mouth replacing handle; incised decoration around mouth and on shoulder. H 30.
 Bibliography: SCE IV. IA 166, fig. 82·4, fig. L1·2; Buchholz and Karageorghis (1973), 145, no. 1495.
 Cyprus Museum, Nicosia. Vasiliko T 1/4.

42 Beaked jug, Red Polished ware
Early Bronze Age (2300–2075 BC)
Philia, Vasiliko, Tomb 1; Department of Antiquities excavations.
Ovoid body, short neck and long beaked spout; handle from mouth to shoulder. H 30.
 Bibliography: SCE IV. IA 166, fig. 82·25, fig. L1·5; Buchholz and Karageorghis (1973), 145, no. 1498.
 Cyprus Museum, Nicosia. Vasiliko T 1/12.

43 Spouted bowl with handle, Red-on-White ware
Early Bronze Age (2300–2075 BC)
Philia, Vasiliko, Tomb 1; Department of Antiquities excavations.
Body decorated with horizontal and vertical stripes in red on a white ground. H 16·8; D 15·3.
 Bibliography: SCE IV. 1A 172, fig. 50·5; Buchholz and Karageorghis (1973), 145, no. 1499.
 Cyprus Museum, Nicosia. Vasiliko T 1/50.

44 Terracotta cult vessel, Red Polished ware
Early Bronze Age (2075–2000 BC)
Vounous, Tomb 160, Chamber B; British excavations.
Deep bowl with rounded sides and flat base. Handle on one side shaped like a sword hilt. On the rim two bulls' heads, a bird's head and two pairs of spoon-like projections. Incised decoration on vessel and protomes (attachments). H 18·2; D 17.
 Bibliography: Stewart (1950), 209f., no. 12, pls. 24, 91B, 92A; Buchholz and Karageorghis (1973), 146, no. 1522.
 Cyprus Museum, Nicosia.

42

44

45

48   50

45 Deep bowl, Red Polished ware
Early Bronze Age (2000–1900 BC)
Phaneromeni, Tomb 24B; American excavations.
Deep conical body, plain rim with rounded edge. Two
opposed large vertical rectangular lugs at rim, apparently
rising from it, but tops not preserved; rim partially preserved. Incised decoration: horizontal bands of hatched
zig-zags, double zig-zag, joined lozenges filled with dots,
short lines and circles; groups of short horizontal lines
below each lug. Repaired and restored. H 33·6; D 17·5.

The soft fabric, deep incised decoration, impractical
shape and opposing spouts set above the rim, all suggest a
ritual function possibly associated with funerary rites. This
early Red Polished pottery with incised decoration has
never been recorded from a settlement. Though related to
the Red Polished series of the Troodos range, its southern
distribution is quite restricted.

Kourion House Museum. Ph/P 34.

46 Copper axe
Early Bronze Age (2300–2075 BC)
Vasilia, Alonia; Department of Antiquities excavations.
Flat and wedge-shaped. Broken at top and bottom. L 16.
Bibliography: Karageorghis, *BCH* XC (1966), 328, fig. 72.
Cyprus Museum, Nicosia. 1965/V-3/8.

47 Copper dagger
Early Bronze Age (2300–2075 BC)
Vasilia, Alonia; Department of Antiquities excavations.
Relatively long tang with single rivet. Leaf-shaped blade
with broad shoulders. Tip of tang broken. L 26.
Bibliography: Karageorghis, *BCH* XC (1966), 328, fig. 73.
Cyprus Museum, Nicosia. 1965/V-3/7.

48 Bronze dagger
Early Bronze Age (2300–2075 BC)
Vasilia.

Willow-shaped blade with broad mid-rib. Rat-tail tang with button terminal. L 30·2.

An exceptionally large and heavy weapon.

Bibliography: Catling (1964), 56, fig. 1·1, pl. 2.b; Buchholz and Karageorghis (1973), 170f, no. 1872.

Cyprus Museum, Nicosia. 1937/III-31/2.

49 Bronze dagger
Early Bronze Age (2300–2075 BC)
Probably from Vasilia.
Leaf-shaped blade with strong central rib; rat-tail tang with button terminal. L 36·5.

Bibliography: Karageorghis, *BCH* LXXXIV (1960), 245, fig. 3, Catling (1964), 56; Buchholz and Karageorghis (1973), 170, no. 1870.

Cyprus Museum, Nicosia. 1959/IV–20/3.

50 Bronze awl
Early Bronze Age (2300–2075 BC)
Probably from Vasilia.
Long blade rectangular in section, pointed at one end and square at the other. Stamped linear sign on blade. L. 26.

Bibliography: Karageorghis, *BCH* LXXXIV (1960), 244, fig. 3; Buchholz and Karageorghis (1973), 170, no. 1869.

Cyprus Museum, Nicosia. 1959/IV–20/2.

51, 52 Two gold hair ornaments
Early Bronze Age (2000–1900 BC)
Lapithos, Tomb 406a/25, 26, American excavations.
Triangular; each rolled into a tubular form and decorated in repoussé with zig-zag lines and dots. L 5.

These are rolled up differently, evidently to secure curls on either side of the head, possibly in imitation of a Minoan hairstyle. Bronze versions from Vounous date from about 2100–2075 BC.

Bibliography: Grace, *AJA* XLIV (1940), 44, nos. 24, 25, pl. 12 (misnumbered 26 for 24 in illustration); Buchholz and Karageorghis (1973), 168, nos. 1825a–b.

Cyprus Museum, Nicosia.

53 Terracotta model of a ploughing scene, Red Polished ware
Early/Middle Bronze Age (about 1900 BC)
Vounous; Department of Antiquities excavations.
Rectangular table on five legs supports the model. Two teams of oxen draw a plough driven by two ploughmen. Another figure drives an animal and two more hold a trough filled with grain. L 41; W 19: H (legs) 14.

This model is particularly important as it illustrates the use of the ox-drawn plough at this early date in Cyprus. The plough itself, consisting of yoke, beam, handle and share, is similar to that in use today. The principal material must have been wood but it is not clear whether the ploughshare

was of metal as it was by 1200 BC (see no. 145 below).

Bibliography: Dikaios, *Archaeologia* LXXXVIII (1940), 127 ff., special series no. 1, pls. 9a, b, 10a; Buchholz and Karageorghis (1973), 161, no. 1704.

Cyprus Museum, Nicosia.
Illustrated in colour.

54, 55 Two terracotta sanctuary models, Red Polished ware
Early/Middle Bronze Age (about 1900 BC)
Kotchati; purchased.
Tripartite shrines, crowned by three bulls' heads, the central upright taller than the others. A pair of horns project lower down at the front and back from the background.
On the floor stands a female figure facing right with outstretched arms before an amphora. No. 55 is partly broken; woman's arms and neck and handles of amphora missing.
54 W 17·5; H 19; Th (base) 2·5. **55** W 14; H 14; Th (base) 2.

These two sanctuary models are important documents illustrating the early religion of Cyprus. Important elements were the worship of the bull, symbol of fertility, here represented by the three *xoanon* (plank-like) figures wearing bulls' heads, and the cthonic or underworld deities, often depicted as snakes. The worship of the bull is also attested in the prehistoric religions of the Near East and the Aegean but in Cyprus the tradition survived into the Archaic period.

Bibliography: Karageorghis, *RDAC* (1970), 10ff., pls. 1–4.

Cyprus Museum, Nicosia. 1970/IV–28/1, 1970/IV–30/1.
54 illustrated in colour.

56 Painted vase (amphora), Red Polished ware
Early/Middle Bronze Age (1950–1850 BC)
Paphos district, Polis tis Chrysochou region.
Ovoid body standing on three legs with handles from rim to shoulder. Body covered with white paint, leaving vertical wavy lines in red from rim to shoulder. H 35·5; D 32·7.

Red polished vessels with white painted decoration are rare and the use of white paint is probably due to foreign influence either from Crete or Western Asia.

Bibliography: Karageorghis, *BCH* XCVIII (1974), 826, fig. 4.

Cyprus Museum, Nicosia. 1973/XII–12/1.

57 Necklace of faience beads
Early/Middle Bronze Age (about 1950–1850 BC)
Kalavassos; Cyprus Archaeological Survey
Cyprus Museum, Nicosia. CS 2434/106.

58 Necklace of paste beads
Early/Middle Bronze Age (about 1950–1850 BC)
Kalavassos; Cyprus Archaeological Survey
Cyprus Museum, Nicosia. CS 2434/76.

The Middle Bronze Age

With the absence of any major upheaval, the transition from Early to Middle Bronze Age is arbitrarily linked, north and east of the Troodos range, to the appearance of a pottery style known as 'White Painted II'. The carefully burnished vessels are decorated with dark paint applied in linear motifs direct to a light background. In the south, a vigorous monochrome tradition (as no. 70) replaced an earlier incised style (no. 45), but with few exceptions this new period is merely an extension of the Early Bronze Age, with a shift in settlement patterns.

Occupation of the island was now complete, excepting the most mountainous regions. For the first time since the end of the Chalcolithic era we have a balanced view of Cypriote culture. Settlements and their adjoining cemeteries have been uncovered at Alambia, Episkopi and Kalopsidha, revealing a well organised quasi-urban society with specialization in metallurgy, as seen at Ambelikou. Houses with large rectangular rooms were built of mud-brick or *pisé* set on stone foundations. Roofs were probably flat, and the floors, usually of trodden earth, were littered with domestic items: pottery, corn grinding equipment, stone tools, and some metal objects. The lighter side of life is suggested by a number of stones marked with shallow depressions arranged in spirals or parallel rows, and interpreted as Cypriote versions of Egyptian board games.

Although burial customs remained unchanged, the increase of weapons in the tombs towards the close of the period might indicate a degree of instability, further emphasized by the construction of fortresses. All, with one exception, were less suited to repulse a foreign incursion than to promote internecine warfare. This state of affairs was probably caused by an increasing degree of regionalization—suggested by differing pottery styles—coupled with an expanding population that put pressure on the dwindling supplies of arable land and water.

A broad distribution of pottery types suggests an island-wide system of exchange developed in accordance with overseas trade, ever increasing as the period matured. Cyprus was breaking free of her insularity, looking to the Levant, and through the adroitness of the inhabitants of those east coast

56

57   58

settlements near future urban centres, she initiated her role as trading emporium of the Late Bronze Age. [s. s.]

59 Terracotta idol, Red Polished ware
Middle Bronze Age (1900–1800 BC)
Akaki. Purchased.
Plank-shaped body with separate arms and legs. Nose and eyebrows in relief. Incised dots and line for necklace around neck and on arms. W 8·4; H 22·2.
Bibliography: Dikaios, *RDAC* (1937–9), 201, pl. 41·3; *SCE* IV. IB, 154, no. 5, fig. 16.9; Buchholz and Karageorghis (1973), 161, no. 1717.
Cyprus Museum, Nicosia. 1938/II–14/1.

60 Terracotta idol, Red Polished ware
Middle Bronze Age (1900–1725 BC)
Unknown provenance; given by Commandant Hubbard of Kyrenia.
Plank-shaped figure with elaborate incised decoration on front and back indicating necklace and a short tunic with decorated hemline. Nose modelled, eyes shown by concentric circles and ears pierced twice. W 9·7; H 26·2.
Bibliography: Karageorghis, *BCH* LXXXVIII (1964), 294, fig. 8; *SCE* IV. IA, fig. 93·2.
Cyprus Museum, Nicosia. 1963/IV–20/12.

61 Terracotta idol, Red Polished ware
Middle Bronze Age (1850–1800 BC)
Lapithos, Tomb 307b; Swedish excavations.
Plank-shaped figure of woman wearing a long robe girdled at the waist with elaborate incised decoration of hatched triangles and lozenges. She is holding a child evidently wrapped in a cloth and lying in a cradle which forms an arch over its head. H 17·71.
Bibliography: *SCE* I, 65, no. 13, pl. 19.
Cyprus Museum, Nicosia.

62 Terracotta female figurine, Red Polished ware
Middle Bronze Age (1900–1725 BC)
Margi.
Woman with prominent breasts seated on a stool and holding a child on her knees. Incised decoration on her head, neck and body indicating a necklace and a garment. Incomplete; stool mostly missing. H 12·2.

60

62

Figures in the round are rare in Middle Bronze Age Cyprus, although plank-shaped idols as nos. 59–61 are quite common. This may be an early illustration of the 'mother and child' theme which was to become popular in Cyprus in later periods.

Bibliography: Karageorghis, *BCH* XCV (1971), 344, fig. 20.

Cyprus Museum, Nicosia. 1970/VI–26/6.

63 Multiple vessel, Red Polished ware
Middle Bronze Age (1900–1800 BC)
Vounous, Tomb 48; Cyprus Museum excavations.

63

Four small hemispherical bowls. Tall ladder-like handle with three rectangular openings crowned by a female figure holding a child. Incised linear decoration on handle and figure. H 46.

Bibliography: Dikaios, *Archaeologia* LXXXVIII (1940), 95, no. 2, pls. 27d, 30b; Buchholz and Karageorghis (1973), 161, no. 1713.

Cyprus Museum, Nicosia.

64 Spherical box (pyxis), Red Polished ware.
Middle Bronze Age (1900–1800 BC)
Vounous, Tomb 2; Department of Antiquities excavations.

64

On the shoulder on either side of the flat lid two plank-shaped idols, one holding a child in its arms. Incised linear decoration on vessel and figures. H 19; D 22.

Bibliography: Dikaios, *Archaeologia* LXXXVIII (1940), 7, no. 91, pl. 36a; Buchholz and Karageorghis (1973), 146, no. 1520.

Cyprus Museum, Nicosia.

65 Multiple vessel, Red Polished ware.
Middle Bronze Age (1900–1800 BC)
Polemidhia.

Three small hemispherical bowls. Each has two pairs of lug handles joined together by bars and is supported by a long stem. All three stems stand on a circular base. H 21; D (bowls) 9–10·3.

This vessel is certainly Cypriote but the shape is Cycladic. One example from the island of Naxos has spouted bowls and has been tentatively identified as a lamp. It is not

65

67

impossible that this piece served a similar purpose, the wick being looped over the projections.

Bibliography: Karageorghis, *BCH* XCVI (1972), 1030, fig. 39.

Limasol Museum. 523/4.

66 Terracotta animal, Red Polished ware
Middle Bronze Age (1900–1725 BC)
Pyla region.

Quadruped with a panier on its back. Incised linear decoration forming zig-zag bands. Partly restored. L 21; H 11.

Bibliography: Karageorghis, *BCH* LXXXIII (1963), 340, fig. 23; Buchholz and Karageorghis (1973), 146, no. 1523.

Cyprus Museum, Nicosia. 1962/IV–17/13.

67 Terracotta bull, Black Polished ware
Middle Bronze Age (1900–1725 BC)
Soloi.

Squat, plump body with short legs and a pair of long horns. Suspension loop on the back of the neck, incised circles for eyes and raised linear decoration on body. L 17·5; H 13.

Bibliography: Buchholz and Karageorghis (1973), 148, no. 1525.

Cyprus Museum, Nicosia. 1943/1–20/1.

68 Terracotta animal, Black Polished ware
Middle Bronze Age (1900–1725 BC)
Unknown provenance.

Quadruped with long neck, small horned head, short tail and four stumpy legs; loop handle from the back of the neck to the shoulder and suspension loop under the neck; incised linear decoration. L 19: H 15·3.

Bibliography: Buchholz and Karageorghis (1973), 148, no. 1526.

Cyprus Museum, Nicosia. A545 (misprinted in publication).

69, 70 Red Polished Mottled ware
Middle Bronze Age (1900–1725 BC)
Red Polished mottled ware is characteristic of the Middle Bronze Age in southern Cyprus. Gone are the exotic shapes and elaborate incised designs of the earlier Red Polished vessels (e.g. nos. 44, 45) in favour of well-made, utilitarian types, for cemeteries and settlements alike.

69 Tripod dish
Phaneromeni, Tomb 23A; American excavations.

Three flat, rectangular legs, supporting a shallow bowl with flat bottom, straight flaring sides, flattened edge. Interior is worn and somewhat convex. Two opposed pairs of horizontal pointed lugs rising vertically from rim. Undecorated. Repaired and restored. H 17; D 32.

Kourion House Museum. Ph/P33.

70 Jug
Phaneromeni, Tomb 25C; American excavations.

Flat base, globular body, narrow conical neck, round spout. Flaring rim, vertical handle, oval in section, from mid-neck to upper body, with four large hemispherical knobs at mid-body. Relief decoration: horizontal band at neckline, broken at handle. H 43; D 35.

Bibliography: Karageorghis, *BCH* CI (1977), 747, fig. 72.
Kourion House Museum. Ph/P 149.

71 Spherical box (pyxis), White Painted ware
Middle Bronze Age (1900–1800 BC)
Vounous, Tomb 64; French excavations.

71

A pair of loop handles on the shoulder and, at each end, a horse protome (attachment) surmounted by a rider. Cross-hatched and linear designs painted in red on a buff ground. Broken and mended; partly restored. Lid missing. L 39·5; H 23·5.

Bibliography: Schaeffer (1936), 35, no. 138, pl. 22·2; Buchholz and Karageorghis (1973), 150, no. 1562.
Cyprus Museum, Nicosia.

72 Terracotta idol, White Painted ware
Middle Bronze Age (1725–1625 BC)
Ayia Paraskevi; Cyprus archaeological survey.
Bearded figure with plank-shaped body and separate arms and legs. Large ears pierced twice. Nose in relief. Details on head, chest, arms and legs painted in red with bands and dots and the lower part of the body covered with solid red paint. Lower part of legs missing; left ear broken. H 34.

Bibliography: Karageorghis, *BCH* XCVIII (1974), 838, fig. 22.
Cyprus Museum, Nicosia. CS 2028/1.
Illustrated in colour.

73 Terracotta idol, White Painted ware
Middle Bronze Age (1725–1625 BC)
Unknown provenance.
Plank-shaped body, long neck; ugly face with prominent nose; large mouth shown by deep incision; cavities for

eyes and nostrils; large ears pierced twice. Arms and legs rendered separately with fingers and toes incised. Left hand held up towards the chin; right arm across body. Decorated with black bands forming a chequer pattern. Paint partly worn away. H 18·7.

Bibliography: Karageorghis, *BCH* XCIX (1975), 812, fig. 21.
Cyprus Museum, Nicosia. 1974/IV–17/1.

73

74

74 Multiple vessel, White Painted ware
Middle Bronze Age (1725–1625 BC)
Lapithos, Vrysi tou Barba, Tomb 21; Cyprus Museum excavations.
A pair of small round beaked jugs, each on three legs with a suspension hole at the neck are joined together at their shoulders by the widespread legs of a human figure whose arms are outstretched with the hands on the handles. Bands, zig-zags and dots, some forming a chequer pattern, decorate the figure and vessels. L 10·4; H 11·5.
Bibliography: Gjerstad (1926), 163, h. 1, fig. p. 160; Buchholz and Karageorghis (1973), 149, no. 1550.
Cyprus Museum, Nicosia. A 907.

75 Animal shaped vessel (askos), White Painted ware
Middle Bronze Age (1725–1625 BC)
Unknown provenance.
Cylindrical body with ram's head at one end and beaked spout at the other. Stands on four short feet with basket handle. Decorated in red with horizontal, vertical and zig-zag bands, and lattice work pattern on body. L 14·8; H 10·5.
Cyprus Museum, Nicosia. A 920.

76 Ring vase, White Painted ware
Middle Bronze Age (1725–1625 BC)
Lapithos, Vrysi tou Barba, Tomb 50; Cyprus Museum excavations.
Ring vase on four feet with tall basket horned handle and tubular spout. String holes on spout, handle and ring.

Decorated with bands and circles in red forming zig-zags and lattice work patterns. L 10·5; H 11·7; D 10·7.
Bibliography: Gjerstad (1926), 163, g. 1, fig. p. 160; Buchholz and Karageorghis (1973), 149, no. 1554.
Cyprus Museum, Nicosia. A 908.

77 Jug, Red-on-Black ware
Middle Bronze Age (1725–1625 BC)
Unknown provenance.
Squat spherical body, flat base, wide cylindrical neck. Handle with knob at top rim to shoulder. Decoration in red: groups of encircling bands between chevron zig-zag pattern on neck; hatched lozenges on shoulder with encircling bands below crossed by vertical lines at intervals forming groups of lattice work. H 26; D 12·5.
This ware is found mainly in eastern Cyprus, especially in the Karpas peninsula.
Bibliography: Buchholz and Karageorghis (1973), 148, no. 1538.
Cyprus Museum, Nicosia. A 960.

78 Kamares ware cup
Middle Bronze Age (1900–1800 BC)
Karmi, Tomb 11/b; Australian excavations.
Tall conical cup on flat base widening out to everted rim. Strap handle. Black painted surface with dog-tooth pattern reserved in the buff of the clay around the base. White painted circles bisected by red horizontal band around rim and upper body of vessel. Below, on body, both inside and out, four white crosses. H 9; D 8·5.
This vase was imported from Crete where Kamares ware is the fine pottery of the first Middle Minoan palaces (2000–1700 BC). It is thrown on the potters' wheel, often eggshell

78

thin, with the ornaments painted, as here, in white and other brilliant colours on the black ground.

Bibliography: Stewart, *Op Ath* IV (1963), 202, no. 6, fig. 8, pl. 7 a–d; Buchholz and Karageorghis (1973), 150, no. 1573.

Cyprus Museum, Nicosia.

79 Bronze dress pin

Middle Bronze Age (1900–1625 BC)
Unknown provenance.

Knot-headed type. Short shaft with the head made of thin wire around the top of the shaft and forming a tight looped coil above it. L 6.

The local metal industry, after a spectacular debut (nos. 46–50 from Vasilia) which resulted in the perfection of a limited range of tool and weapon types, remained stagnant until well into the Late Bronze Age. Archaic designs and outdated techniques were the hallmark of the Middle Bronze Age. For a country so rich in copper, the smiths were surprisingly bound by tradition, ignoring the influence provided by the more sophisticated technology of imports or foreign influenced objects (as nos. 80–81).

Bibliography: Buchholz and Karageorghis (1973), 108, no. 1812.

Cyprus Museum, Nicosia. Met. 1362.

80, 81 Two bronze axes

Middle Bronze Age (1900–1625 BC)
Unknown provenance.

Shaft-hole type with cylindrical ribbed sockets and long blades. L 19 (both).

These axes are cast in moulds and the examples so far found in Cyprus are remarkably alike. They may therefore have been made locally, more probably by a foreign smith

80

using moulds brought with him rather than by Cypriote workmen, since a considerable amount of skill is required for their production. On present evidence Cypriote bronze-smiths would not have been capable of reaching the required standard so early.

Bibliography: Catling (1964), 66; Karageorghis, *BCH* XCII (1968), 276, fig. 29; Buchholz and Karageorghis (1973), 171, nos. 1878, 1879.

Cyprus Museum, Nicosia. **80** 1958/II-8/1; **81** 1967/III-10/1.

82 Strainer jug, Red Polished ware

Middle/Late Bronze Age (1650–1600 BC)
Phaneromeni, Settlement A; American excavations.

Thin walled with a large hole on one side of the shoulder. Ovoid body and round base. Conical neck, round spout,

82

flaring rim and strainer with four holes over the end of the spout. Vertical handle from centre of neck to shoulder. Decorated in relief: impressed bands encircling hole and entire body in an interlocking pattern. Two shallow incised Xs on neck and two vertical rows of crude punctures. Finger impressions on handle. Repaired and restored. H 55; D 39.

Red Polished ware of this late variety evolved naturally from Red Polished Mottled ware (as nos. 69, 70) and remains the most functional of ceramic types at Phaneromeni. Both Blue Core and this later Red Polished ware were favoured, probably due to their extreme hardness, for the manufacture of medium to large closed vessels.

Kourion House Museum. Ph/P 308.

83, 84 Episkopi ware

Middle/Late Bronze Age (1650–1600 BC)
Phaneromeni, settlement A; American excavations.

panel with reserved angular spirals on upper body; vertical bands of multiple straight, zig-zag, and broken lines on lower body. Nearly half preserved. Restored. H 12; D 19.
Kourion House Museum. Ph/P 217.

83

85

Episkopi ware, with Blue Core and later Red Polished ware, was discovered in great quantities smashed on the floors of the settlement at Phaneromeni (Episkopi), burnt near the beginning of the Late Bronze Age about 1600 BC. It developed in the Middle Bronze Age from an undecorated prototype, and is apparently restricted to the neighbourhood of Phaneromeni, with rare occurrences further east.

83 Juglet

Squat ovoid body and round base. Narrow neck with beaked spout. Vertical handle from rim to shoulder and two vertical lugs at the middle of the neck and on the neckline. Incised decoration: on upper body panel with triangles filled with punctured bands and groups of parallel lines arranged symmetrically; four-pointed tool used for horizontal lines on neck; deep vertical incisions on handle. H 22·3; D 12·5.
Kourion House Museum. Ph/P 164.

84 Bowl

Round base, deep ovoid body, plain rim; horizontal ledge lug, pierced twice (?) at rim. Incised decoration: punctured

85 Tankard, Blue Core ware

Middle/Late Bronze Age (1650–1600 BC)
Phaneromeni, Settlement A; American excavations.
Globular body, round base, plain vertical rim. One handle attachment preserved on upper body and remains of a second opposite, but the latter was not used. Decoration incised with a three-pointed tool: two horizontal zig–zags divided by straight horizontal band on upper body; horizontal band at neckline, large horizontal zig–zag on neck. Repaired and restored. H 21·3; D 15·1.

Blue Core ware shows a steady development throughout the Middle Bronze Age. Its place of greatest popularity, and possible origin, is near Paphos.
Kourion House Museum. Ph/P 203.

53 Terracotta ploughing scene,
about 1900 BC.

54 Terracotta shrine model,
about 1900 BC.

72 Terracotta idol,
1725–1625 BC.

170 Terracotta figurine,
1450–1225 BC.

86 Silver bowl from Enkomi,
1400–1375 BC.

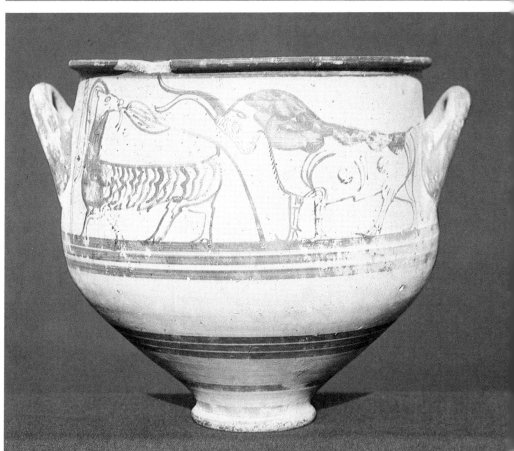

98 Mycenaean vessel
from Enkomi,
1300–1230 BC.

102 The Ingot God
from Enkomi,
1200–1100 BC.

107 Faience rhyton from Kition,
1300–1225 BC.

155 Gold and enamel sceptre from Kourion,
1100–1050 BC.

193 Terracotta goddess with uplifted arms,
1050–950 B.C.

269 Terracotta warrior,
700–600 BC.

227, 228 Open-work ivory plaques from Salamis,
about 700 BC.

The Late Bronze Age

Two main factors which gave Cyprus an important place in Mediterranean history were her geographical position between the orient and occident and her wealth in copper. In the second half of the second millennium BC, the period known as the Late Bronze Age, they particularly dictated the island's destiny. After the upheavals that disturbed the eastern Mediterranean before the final establishment of peace towards 1500 BC, Cyprus found herself in the centre of active commercial relations between the Aegean and the Near East. The Mycenaeans (from mainland Greece) were attracted by the copper and also used the harbour towns of the east and south coasts of the island in their trade with the Near East. Goods from Egypt and the Near East flooded the rich market of Cyprus, where large quantities of Mycenaean pottery (either imported from the Aegean or made locally by Mycenaean craftsmen) could also be found. Copper and other goods were sent to Egypt, as we are informed by the correspondence between the King of Alashia (which has been identified as Cyprus) and the Pharaoh, as tribute for the role the Egyptians played in keeping the peace in the eastern Mediterranean. This is the heyday of the cosmopolitan coastal towns such as Enkomi, Kition, Hala Sultan Tekké and Maroni.

Towards 1200 BC, after the destruction and abandonment of the main towns of the Peloponnese, the first Achaean immigrants arrived from that area to settle in the flourishing commercial centres of Cyprus, bringing with them elements of their own culture, which was gradually to become the basis of Cypriote civilisation. This colonization was a very slow, peaceful process, achieved through successive waves of newcomers from the Aegean, and by the end of the twelfth century Cyprus may be considered part of the Hellenic world, where Greek was spoken and Greek culture was familiar. This was a troubled period in the Mediterranean, with adventurers known as the 'Peoples of the Sea' roaming the coasts. Cyprus did not remain unaffected.

The Achaeans caused serious cultural changes in the island, introducing new pottery styles and religious traditions including the 'horns of consecration'. However the Near Eastern connections of Cyprus were not forgotten. Large temples and other public buildings, constructed of ashlar blocks, were built within the 'cyclopean walls' at Enkomi and Kition where gods and goddesses connected with metallurgy were worshipped (e.g. no. 102). Characteristic products of the fourteenth to twelfth centuries are jewellery, ivories and faience vessels that show a mixture of Syrian, Egyptian and Aegean (both Mycenaean and Cretan, that is Minoan) elements.

The final phase of the Late Bronze Age, dating from 1125 to 1050 BC, is sometimes described as 'Protogeometric' since, as a whole, the material culture anticipates that of the succeeding Geometric period. The population now dwindled, but in the closing years of the twelfth century a fresh wave of Achaean immigrants, including Cretans, provided new impetus.

Mycenaean tombs with long *dromoi* (entrance passages) are found in cemeteries alongside the native Cypriote types. New to Cyprus too are the terracottas with wheel-made bodies, including the Cretan goddess with uplifted arms (nos. 186–187), and Proto-White Painted pottery typical of the period. The latter employs for the most part shapes and ornaments of Aegean origin, sometimes specifically Cretan. Nonetheless Cyprus maintains her ties with the Levant whence comes the bichrome technique. This now makes its appearance together with certain shapes such as pilgrim vessels (e.g. no. 181) which are both imported and locally made. Generally the Cypriote Proto-White Painted and Proto-Bichrome wares are of far higher quality both in their manufacture and their decoration than their Sub-Minoan and Sub-Mycenaean contemporaries. Some forms like the bird or duck askoi (e.g. nos. 100, 142), also found in the Greek world, are evidently a Cypriote invention.

Although, as we shall see, there was a catastrophe in the early eleventh century, some sites illustrate the years to 1050 BC. Kition was quickly rebuilt, and a tomb of the first half of the eleventh century at Salamis shows that the settlement here overlapped for a short time with that at Enkomi. Palaepaphos was continuously occupied from the Bronze into the Iron Age. Our knowledge of the 'Protogeometric' period increases as more finds come to light.

A natural phenomenon, perhaps an earthquake, in the second quarter of the eleventh century caused the destruction of several Late Bronze Age towns including Kition and Enkomi, the latter being almost totally abandoned. The subsequent establishment of new towns such as Salamis, Paphos and Soloi survived in mythical tradition as the foundation of cities in Cyprus by the heroes of the Trojan War.

[V. K. and V. A. T.-B.]

Enkomi

The east coast of Cyprus, with a natural harbour and a rich and fertile hinterland, has been the most prosperous part of the island throughout her history. Already in the seventeenth century BC a small community was established there and was destined to become one of the main Late Bronze Age centres in Cyprus during the fourteenth and thirteenth centuries BC. Enkomi is the name of the modern village, west of which the ancient site is located. It was discovered by a French expedition under Professor C. F. A. Schaeffer and was excavated jointly by the French team and the Department of Antiquities of Cyprus. The British Museum in 1890 and the Swedish Cyprus expedition in the thirties excavated tombs at this site.

From the inner harbour of Enkomi copper was exported to the east and west (the copper ore having been brought from inland) and in one of her temples an 'Ingot god' (standing on a base in the form of a copper ingot) was worshipped (no. 102). The town was fortified with 'cyclopean walls' towards 1200 BC and was adorned with spacious 'places' and temples built of ashlar blocks. A large part of the town has been uncovered revealing a unique town plan. The streets cross each other at right angles and connect the various gates of the city wall with one another.

Rich tombs were excavated in the courtyards of some houses. They produced gold, ivory, alabaster and bronze objects, and magnificently decorated Mycenaean pottery. Some of these tomb-groups (excavated in 1890) are now in the British Museum. Incribed tablets of baked clay, bearing texts in the Cypro-Minoan syllabary have also been found (e.g. no. 147) as well as a number of the writing implements or styli (no. 146). [V. K.]

86 Silver bowl, inlaid with gold and niello
Late Bronze Age (1400–1375 BC)
Enkomi, Tomb 2/7; French excavations.
Hemispherical bowl with a wish-bone handle. Decorated in gold and niello with six bulls' heads alternating with lotus flowers. Below, a frieze of arcaded rosettes. There is a series of dots around the rim. H 6; D 15·7.

The technique of inlaying one metal with another was known in Syria and Egypt in the twentieth century BC and reached the Mycenaean world in the middle of the second millennium. A similar bowl to this was found in a contemporary tomb at Dendra in the Argolid (southern Greece). Bowls with wish-bone handles are common in Cypriote pottery and an undecorated silver version, also from Enkomi, is now in the British Museum (GR 1897. 4–1·300). It is just possible that the decorated Enkomi and Dendra bowls were made by the same craftsman, but there seems to be no reason to doubt that the Cypriote bowl is a local product.

Bibliography: Schaeffer (1952), 128f., 379 ff., no. 4·207, pls. 116, C–D, figs. 118–122; Strong (1966), 51f., pl. 7b; Buchholz and Karageorghis (1973), 158, no. 1684, col. pl. 4.

Cyprus Museum, Nicosia.

Illustrated in colour.

87 Gold pectoral (breast ornament)

Late Bronze Age (1400–1230 BC)

Enkomi, Tomb 2; French excavations.

Elliptical with perforated ends. Stamped decoration showing a pair of confronted sphinxes standing either side of a palmette. Dotted rosettes above and below and a dotted border. L 17·5; W 10.

This was discovered on the chest of the skeleton lying underneath at right angles to a rectangular ornament with identical decoration, perhaps from the same stamp. In shape it closely resembles the mouth-piece (94), but there is no indication of the mouth. Indeed, it would be more suitable as a breast ornament, as indicated by its find-spot.

Bibliography: Schaeffer (1952), 127f., no. 4·202, pl. 24·1; Buchholz and Karageorghis (1973), 166, no. 1775.

Cyprus Museum, Nicosia.

88 Gold necklace

Late Bronze Age (1450–1225 BC)

Enkomi, Tomb 10; Department of Antiquities excavations.

Fourteen globular ribbed beads alternating with fourteen tubular links made of gold wire wound into a spiral and soldered. L (of beads) 1·2; D (of beads) 0·5.

Globular ribbed beads are common in Cyprus and the type is also found in the Near East and the Aegean. The spiral links, however, are difficult to parallel outside the island.

Bibliography: *Enkomi* I, 373, no. 165, IIIa, pl. 208/25.

Cyprus Museum, Nicosia.

89 Mycenaean vessel (amphoroid krater)

Late Bronze Age (1400–1300 BC)

Enkomi, Tomb 10; Department of Antiquities excavations.

In the shoulder frieze bulls are leaping over rocky ground, three on each side, one with head turned back. Between them stand human figures, two on one side and one on the other. Glazed foot and neck, and stripes around the lower part of the body. H 43·5; D 31·7.

89

Bibliography: *Enkomi* I, 367, no. 23, III A, pls. 203–4; 204a, 223–4; Buchholz and Karageorghis (1973), 152, no. 1620 (mistakenly numbered as 200).

Cyprus Museum, Nicosia.

90 Terracotta 'Snake House', Plain White ware, handmade

Late Bronze Age (about 1400–1200 BC)

Enkomi, Tomb 10; Department of Antiquities excavations.

Tube-shaped at one end and open at the other with a flat base and three perforations along each of the long sides and upper part. L 37; W 11; H 14.

Formerly seen as the home of a snake, a symbol of the underworld deities in Cyprus, it is now identified as a heating element.

Bibliography: *Enkomi* IIIa, no. 821, pl. 150/15; Karageorghis *RDAC* (1972), 109 ff.

Cyprus Museum, Nicosia.

91 Mycenaean vessel (amphoroid krater)

Late Bronze Age (1400–1375 BC)

Enkomi, Tomb 17; Swedish excavations.

On one side a chariot driving to the right. Before it stands a figure holding scales, and a warrior. In the field above is a bull and a stylised bird; below, a tree and a flower. Glazed foot and rim, band around the bottom of the neck. H 37·5.

This vase is known as the 'Zeus Krater' since the principal scene has been interpreted as Zeus, holding the scales of

91

93

fate, before warriors departing for battle, which illustrates a passage in Homer's *Iliad*.

Bibliography: SCE I, 543, no. 1, pl. 120. 3–4; Buchholz and Karageorghis (1973), 152, no. 1621.

Cyprus Museum, Nicosia.

92 Gold finger-ring

Late Bronze Age (1450–1225 BC)

Enkomi, Tomb 18; Swedish excavations.

Stirrup-shaped hoop with elliptical bezel. Engraved on the bezel is a bull walking to the left towards a crescent and disc. Dotted border. D 2·3.

Bibliography: SCE I, 555, side chamber no. 11, pls. 88, 145; Pierides (1971), 20, pl. 10·3–4.

Cyprus Museum, Nicosia.

93 Gold finger-ring

Late Bronze Age (1450–1225 BC)

Enkomi, Tomb 18; Swedish excavations.

Stirrup-shaped hoop with oval bezel. On the bezel, in relief, is a lion walking to the right with its head turned back. D 2·6.

In shape these finger-rings owe a debt to Egypt and not to the Mycenaean world where the bezel was set at right angles to the hoop. The decoration is either of Cypriote or

Mycenaean inspiration but the rings must be local products.

Bibliography: SCE I, 553, no. 62, pls. 88, 145·22–23; Pierides (1971), 20, pl. 10·1–2; Buchholz and Karageorghis (1973), 167, 490, no. 1784.

Cyprus Museum, Nicosia.

94 Gold mouth-piece

Late Bronze Age (1450–1225 BC)

Enkomi, Tomb 18; Swedish excavations.

Elliptical with perforated corners. Stamped decoration showing, within a dotted border, three spirals at each end. In the centre a design of two series of connected spirals with short dotted lines to indicate the mouth. L 11·3; W 5.

Bibliography: SCE I, 552, no. 37, pl. 88. Pierides (1971), 16, pl. 7·1.

Cyprus Museum, Nicosia.

95 Gold diadem

Late Bronze Age (1450–1225 BC)

Enkomi, Tomb 18; Swedish excavations.

Rectangular with rounded ends each perforated twice. Stamped decoration showing two rows of double palmettes enclosed by dots within a dotted border. L 21·8; W 4·5.

These diadems are usually found in tombs. Their form is Asiatic but their decoration is often of Mycenaean inspiration.

Bibliography: SCE I, 551, no. 1, pl. 88. Pierides (1971), 15 f., pl. 6·1.

Cyprus Museum, Nicosia.

96 Gold diadem

Late Bronze Age (1450–1225 BC)

Enkomi, Tomb 18; Swedish excavations.

Rectangular with rounded ends each perforated twice.

96

Stamped decoration. Two rows of winged sphinxes seated to the right, flanked by circles. Dotted border. Some perforations broken. L 14·9; W 3·7.

Bibliography: *SCE* I, 554, no. 95, pls. 88, 146·6; Pierides (1971), 15, pl. 5·1.

Cyprus Museum, Nicosia.

97 Glass pomegranate flask
Late Bronze Age (1225–1050 BC)
Enkomi, Tomb 43
H 11·1

Cypriote glass pomegranate flasks, probably used for perfume or oil, differ from their Egyptian counterparts in form and decoration and were probably made in Cyprus itself.

Cyprus Museum, Nicosia. G 91.

98 Mycenaean vessel (bell krater)
Late Bronze Age (1300–1230 BC)
Enkomi, Tomb 19; Swedish excavations.
In the handle frieze on one side a goat walking to the left with head turned back followed by a bull; a tall flower between them. On the other side a bull eats the leaves of a bush. Glazed rim and handles, stripes around lower part of body and foot. H 27.

Bibliography: *SCE* I, 564, no. 66, pl. 118.
Cyprus Museum, Nicosia.
Illustrated in colour

99 Gold pendant
Late Bronze Age (1400–1230 BC)
Probably from Enkomi.
In the form of a pomegranate decorated with triangles of granulation. H 4·7; D 3·2.

99

Bibliography: Buchholz and Karageorghis (1973), 167, no. 1780.
Cyprus Museum, Nicosia. 1954/III–24/1.

100 Vessel in the form of a bird (askos), White Painted Wheel-made ware.
Late Bronze Age (1200–1050 BC)
Enkomi, Tomb; bought from Mr G. Palma of Famagusta.
Spout and basket handle on the back. Disc base. Decorated in red with wings, feathers and eyes depicted. Stripes around body, rim, handle and spout. L 27; H 17.

Vases in this purely local fabric are found alongside Mycenaean vessels. A bird vase in this ware adds further weight to the theory that the shape is a Cypriote invention (cf. no. 142 below).

Bibliography: Dikaios, *RDAC* (1935), 27, pl. 9, 4; Buchholz and Karageorghis (1973), 154, no. 1649.

Cyprus Museum, Nicosia. 1935/XII–24/2.

101 Bronze statuette, 'The Horned God'

Late Bronze Age (1200–1150 BC)

Enkomi, sanctuary of the Horned God; Department of Antiquities excavations.

Male figure dressed in a short kilt and conical cap from which spring two horns. He stands with the left leg slightly advanced, the right arm bent forwards with the palm facing the ground and the left arm bent across the chest with fist clenched. W (across shoulders) 17·5; H 54·2.

This fine statuette has been variously identified as a god or a worshipper. Whoever he is, he is one of the most remarkable finds from twelfth century Cyprus. In style it is close to that of the ivory mirror handles (e.g. no. 134) and it shows Aegean influence in its naturalism and dress. It was probably locally made either by an Aegean craftsman or by a Levantine artisan working for Aegean masters in the island.

Bibliography: Catling (1964), 255f., no. 6, pl. 46; *Enkomi* I, 295, II, 529f., IIIA pls. 138/36, 139–144; Buchholz and Karageorghis (1973), 163, no. 1740.

Cyprus Museum, Nicosia. 1949/V–20/6.

102 Bronze statuette, 'The Ingot God'.

Late Bronze Age (1200–1100 BC)

Enkomi, sanctuary of the Ingot God; French excavations.

Male figure standing on an ingot, his head raised. He wears a close-fitting vest, knee-length apron and conical cap from which spring two short horns. In his right hand he holds a spear ready to thrust and in his left a shield. H 35.

Bibliography: Shaeffer, *AFO* XXI (1965), 59ff., no. 16·15; Schaeffer, *Alasia* I (1971), 506ff., figs. 1–3, pls. 1–7; Buchholz and Karageorghis (1973), 163, no. 1741.

Cyprus Museum, Nicosia.

Illustrated in colour.

103 Bronze chariot group

Late Bronze Age (1200–1100 BC)

Enkomi, bronze foundry; French excavations, 1969.

A four-wheeled cart carries a bull driven by a cowherd. It is accompanied by a cat and a dog who bites the cat's tail. L 8·5; W 6·5; H 10.

This is a religious scene showing the bull being led to sacrifice. Two similar carts carrying bulls are known; the example in the Louvre was probably also of Cypriote manufacture and the third, in a private collection, is virtually identical to the other two.

103

Bibliography: Schaeffer, *Syria* XLVI (1969), 267ff., pls. 18–20, fig. 8.
Cyprus Museum, Nicosia.

104 Bronze statuette

Late Bronze Age (1200–1100 BC)
Enkomi; chance find.
Seated male figure wearing an ankle-length garment with a V-shaped neckline, the folds indicated by incised lines. The left arm rests by the knee and the right is folded across the body onto the lap. Eyes originally inlaid and eyebrows indicated by incised lines. H 7·5.
Bibliography: Catling (1964), 253, no. 1, pl. 45a, b; *Enkomi* II, 779, IIIA pl. 151; Buchholz and Karageorghis (1973), 162, no. 1733.
Cyprus Museum, Nicosia. 1944/II–24/1.

105 Bronze table

Late Bronze Age (1200–1100 BC)
Enkomi, House of Bronzes; French excavations.
Round tray with central circular depression and low rim. Cast in one piece with the four looped feet rivetted onto the underside separately. H 22·5; D 65·5.

This is one of two bronze examples from Enkomi. They probably served as portable hearths like related finds of stucco found on Aegean sites from the end of the Late Bronze Age onwards.
Bibliography: Schaeffer (1936), 87, pls. 39, 4, 40; Catling (1964), 155f., no. 1, pl. 22; Buchholz and Karageorghis (1973), 155, no. 1688.
Cyprus Museum, Nicosia.

106 Terracotta double-headed 'Centaur'.

Late Bronze Age (1100–1050 BC)
Enkomi, Sanctuary of the 'Ingot God'; French excavations.
Animal body with two human heads. The body and heads are decorated in matt orange with bands, stripes, chevrons and semi-circles partly arranged in metopes (panels). Wheel-made cylindrical body and legs. Broken and mended, partly restored. L 25·5; H 3·1; D (body) 15.

105

106

A second, more fragmentary example, also double-headed, was found in the same place. Wheel-made animal statuettes are popular offerings in shrines in Mycenaean Greece from the thirteenth century and in Crete more particularly in the twelfth century. They were introduced to Cyprus by the first wave of Aegean settlers around 1200 BC. Particularly close parallels for both the form and painted decoration are found in Crete (although the Minoan pieces are single-headed). The general type was therefore evidently introduced from Crete along with the 'goddess with uplifted arms'. The two-headed version is probably an Anatolian creation.

Bibliography: Courtois, *Alasia* I (1971), 294ff., no. 40, centaur B, figs. 124–127; Buchholz and Karageorghis (1973), 162, no. 1731.

Cyprus Museum, Nicosia.

Kition

The site of Kition lies under the houses of the modern town of Larnaca, on the south-east coast of Cyprus. It formed part of the chain of coastal towns which flourished during the Late Bronze Age. Other neighbouring towns of the same period are Pyla (to the north-east) and Hala Sultan Tekké (to the south-west). The Bronze Age town has been excavated by the Department of Antiquities of Cyprus since 1969. Previous work (under Sir John Myres and the Swedish Cyprus expedition) uncovered only part of the Iron Age town.

The earliest Late Bronze Age remains date from the thirteenth century, but there are also Early and Middle Bronze Age tombs in the area. In the main excavated part at the northern extremity of the town (Area II) an important sacred area was covered, comprising at least two temples with sacred gardens, dating from the thirteenth century BC. This sacred area became even larger after 1200 BC, with five large temples and sacred gardens. There were workshops for the smelting of copper adjoining and communicating with the temples and the courtyards, illustrating the close relationship between religion and metallurgy, the former controlling the latter; we know that copper was the basis of the island's economy.

Rich tombs have been excavated in the nearby Area I, which produced Near Eastern and Aegean goods, including the famous faience rhyton (no. 107).

Kition has not only produced important architectural monuments, including an impressive 'cyclopean' wall with rectangular bastions, but has also provided much information about the religion of Late Bronze Age Cyprus. [V. K.]

107 Faience vessel (rhyton)
Late Bronze Age (1300–1225 BC)
Kition, outside Tomb 5; Department of Antiquities excavations.
Conical rhyton with thickened rim, and grooved handle from rim to shoulder. Body divided into registers by relief ribs. Faience coated with enamel; decoration inlaid or painted. The two upper registers show hunting scenes and

fleeing animals with tree motifs in the background; upright in lower register. Base and handle missing. H 26·8; D 11·9.

This remarkable work combines Aegean, Syrian and Egyptian elements. The shape and some of the ornaments are Aegean; details of the hunting scene and polychrome decoration are at home in the Levant; other motifs, including the huntsman in a kilt striking an antelope, are Egyptian. It was probably made either in Cyprus itself or in Byblos, a Phoenician city which produced many items showing strong Egyptian influence.

Bibliography: Buchholz and Karageorghis (1973), 157, no. 1671, col. pl. 3; *Kition* I, 116 ff., special series no. 1, pls. A–C, 94–95.

Cyprus Museum, Nicosia.

Illustrated in colour.

108 Ivory disc

Late Bronze Age (1300–1225 BC)

Kition, Tomb 4 and 5; Department of Antiquities excavations. Probably the lid of a circular box. Flat and pierced in the centre for a gold button, now missing. Engraved decoration on one side showing a volute around a central rosette within a decorated border. Fragmentary. D 8·5.

Ivory, the raw material, had to be imported and Cyprus probably obtained hers from Syria. Unfinished pieces from Palaepaphos show that the island had its own workshops producing ivories in the characteristic 'mixed style' under influence from both the Near East and the Aegean.

Bibliography: SCE IV. 1D 611; Buchholz and Karageorghis (1973), 163, no. 1744; *Kition* I, 33, 40, no. 235, pls. 36, 133.

Cyprus Museum, Nicosia.

108

109 Mycenaean shallow bowl

Late Bronze Age (1300–1225 BC)

Kition, Tomb 4 and 5; Department of Antiquities exca-

109

vations. Shallow bowl as no. 122. Decorated in red to dark brown glossy paint. On the inside flying swallows; encircling bands on the outside. Fragmentary, partly restored. H 6; D 19.

Bibliography: Buchholz and Karageorghis (1973), 154, no. 1643; *Kition* I, 24, 38, no. 132, pls. 31, 132.

Cyprus Museum, Nicosia.

110 Ivory disc

Late Bronze Age (1300–1225 BC)

Kition, Tomb 9, lower burial; Department of Antiquities excavations.

Probably the lid of a circular box; engraved decoration on one side showing the head of a lion facing left before a tree within a decorated border. Fragmentary. D 9.

Bibliography: *Kition* I, 44, 61, no. 19, pls. 65, 150.

Cyprus Museum, Nicosia.

110

111 Mycenaean terracotta figurine, the 'psi' type
Late Bronze Age (1300–1230 BC)
Kition, Tomb 9, lower burial. Department of Antiquities excavations.
In the form of the Greek letter ψ (psi). Features indicated in red glossy paint and details of the dress also shown in red with oblique lines over breast and arms and vertical wavy lines on lower part of body. H 6·7.
Bibliography: Kition I, 44, 62, no. 13, pl. 63.
Cyprus Museum, Nicosia.

112 Mycenaean bowl
Late Bronze Age (1300–1225 BC)
Kition, Tomb 9, lower burial; Department of Antiquities excavations.
Deep bowl with S-shaped sides, flat base and wish-bone handle. Decorated in glossy red with a frieze of stylised flowers in the handle zone below the rim and encircling lines around the body inside and out. Red lip and handle. H 8; D 12·5.
Although the fabric is Mycenaean the shape is Cypriote, commonly represented in the local Base Ring ware.
Bibliography: Buchholz and Karageorghis (1973), 153, no. 1639; *Kition* I, 44, 58, no. 12, pls. 54, 143.
Cyprus Museum, Nicosia.

113 Gold finger-ring
Late Bronze Age (1300–1225 BC)
Kition, Tomb 9, upper burial; Department of Antiquities excavations.
Composed of gold wire twisted as double loop-in-loop chain. D 2.
Earrings are made in the same technique (e.g. no. 157). This is a particularly popular technique in Late Bronze Age Cyprus and was probably a local invention.
Bibliography: Kition I, 76, 88f., no. 241, pl. 92.
Cyprus Museum, Nicosia.

114

114 Gold finger-ring
Late Bronze Age (1300–1225 BC)
Kition, Tomb 9, upper burial; Department of Antiquities excavations.
Broad hoop and elliptical bezel. On the bezel engraved decoration showing a bull to the left with trees in the background. D (bezel) 1·6; D (hoop) 1·8.
Bibliography: Buchholz and Karageorghis (1973), 167, no. 1781; *Kition* I, 76, 88, no. 249, pl. 92.
Cyprus Museum, Nicosia.

115 Gold finger-ring
Late Bronze Age (1300–1225 BC)
Kition, Tomb 9, upper burial; Department of Antiquities excavations.
Plain hoop with ovoid revolving gold setting for the faience bezel in the form of a bull's head. Gold wire twisted around the ends of the hoop and threaded through the bezel. L (bezel) 2·3; D (hoop) 2·4.
The swivel ring is an Egyptian creation but by the Late Bronze Age it had been adopted in the Levant, whence it probably reached Cyprus.
Bibliography: Buchholz and Karageorghis (1973), 167, no. 1783; *Kition* I, 79, 88, no. 291, pl. 92.
Cyprus Museum, Nicosia.

116 Gold diadem
Late Bronze Age (1300–1225 BC)
Kition, Tomb 9, upper burial; Department of Antiquities excavations. Rectangular with rounded corners and three perforations at each end; stamped decoration, showing three rows of rosettes. L 26·2; W 3·8.
As nos. 95, 96 above.
Bibliography: Buchholz and Karageorghis (1973), 167, no. 1794 (numbered in error as T9 UB 22); *Kition* I, 79, 88, no. 298, pl. 91.
Cyprus Museum, Nicosia.

117 Pair of gold earrings
Late Bronze Age (1300–1225 BC)
Kition, Tomb 9, upper burial; Department of Antiquities excavations. Hoops of thin wire threaded with bulls' heads stamped from sheet gold. L 3; D of ring 1·5.
Earrings of this type occur first in Cyprus and are probably of local origin. They are quite common, a similar pair comes from Palaepaphos (no. 136).
Bibliography: Buchholz and Karageorghis (1973), 166, no. 1778; *Kition* I, 69f., 88, no. 134, pl. 91.
Cyprus Museum, Nicosia.

118 Gold pendant and beads
Late Bronze Age (1300–1225 BC)

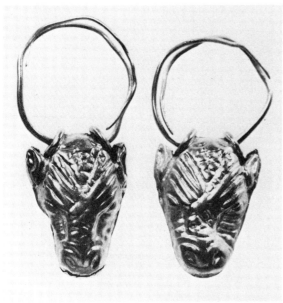

117

118

Aegean. The pendant is similar to the Babylonian cylinder seal on a necklace from Ayios Iakovos (no. 156).

Bibliography: Buchholz and Karageorghis (1973), 167, no. 1791; *Kition* I, 79, 89, no. 293, pl. 92.

Cyprus Museum, Nicosia.

119 Necklace
Late Bronze Age (1300–1225 BC)
Kition, Tomb 9, upper burial; Department of Antiquities excavations.

Composed of 197 glass beads and three faience or paste beads with two bottle-shaped carnelian pendants. L (of beads) 1·2–2·3; D (of beads) 1–1·5.

Bibliography: Kition I, 79f., 92, no. 306, pls. 88, 171.

Cyprus Museum, Nicosia.

120 Ivory box, in the shape of a bath tub
Late Bronze Age (1300–1225 BC)
Kition, Tomb 9, upper burial; Department of Antiquities excavations.

Two small vertical handles on either side and a dowel hole for the lid at the top of one short side. Grooves along the side

120

of the handles and at the top and bottom of the box. L 11·7; W 4·5; H 3·3.

Bibliography: Buchholz and Karageorghis (1973), 163, no. 1742; *Kition* I, 83, 91, no. 354, pls. 87, 170.

Cyprus Museum, Nicosia.

121 Faience bowl
Late Bronze Age (1300–1225 BC)
Kition, Tomb 9, upper burial; Department of Antiquities excavations.

Deep bowl with carinated shoulders and a pair of lug handles. Lower part of body decorated with vertical ribs. H 7·9; D 9.

This belongs to the Levantine group of faience vessels. The shape is particularly common in Western Asia and a number of examples have been found in Cyprus.

Bibliography: Buchholz and Karageorghis (1973), 163, no. 1680; *Kition* I, 75, 92, 110, no. 230, pls. 88, 163.

Cyprus Museum, Nicosia.

Kition, Tomb 9, upper burial; Department of Antiquities excavations.

Cylindrical gold pendant with engraved decoration showing a human figure, two birds, a fish and a tree. There are five gold beads: three globular and two elliptical (one of wire and the other decorated with granulation). Also, one globular faience bead. L (seal) 0·7, (beads) 0·7, 0·8, 1·4; D (faience bead) 0·7.

The beads are of different types: the globular examples are Syrian, the one composed of gold wire (as no. 88 from Enkomi) is a local variety, and the bead with granulation is

121

122 Mycenaean bowl
Late Bronze Age (1300–1225 BC)
Kition, Tomb 9, upper burial; Department of Antiquities excavations.
Shallow conical body, low foot ring and pair of horizontal strap handles at the rim. Decorated in dark red to purple matt paint. On the inside, a spiral in the centre around which is a frieze of fish bordered by a band of zig-zags. Hatched lozenges on the outer zone. On the outside encircling bands. Broken and mended; partly restored. H 4·5; D 17·8.
Bibliography: Buchholz and Karageorghis (1973), 154, no. 1641; *Kition* I, 67, 87, no. 90, pls. 73, 159.
Cyprus Museum, Nicosia.

123 Jug, Bucchero wheel-made ware
Late Bronze Age (1300–1225 BC)
Kition, Tomb 9, upper burial; Department of Antiquities excavations.
Ovoid body, low foot, handle from rim to shoulder. Body decorated with oblique and vertical grooves. Rim restored. H 19·2.
This local pottery was found alongside the Mycenaean vessels.
Bibliography: Kition I, 69, 86, no. 128, pls. 68, 154.
Cyprus Museum, Nicosia.

124–126 Ivories
These three ivories were found together in Temple 4 immediately below a level dating from shortly after 1200 BC. The temple was dedicated to a female goddess and the ivories evidently played a part in the cult. They are the first inscribed pieces of the period to be found. The 'flying leap' of the lion is characteristically Mycenaean while the 'Bes' figure has close parallels from Megiddo in Syria. The pipe may have been used for smoking opium.
124 Ivory 'Bes'
Late Bronze Age (about 1200 BC)

124

126

Kition, Temple 4; Department of Antiquities excavations. Plaque in the form of the Egyptian god 'Bes' engraved on both sides. He wears a feather crown, lion skin and knee-length skirt with a long sash. His right arm is raised to hold a sword against his head. He stands in profile, his knees bent as though running, on a flat base inscribed in the Cypro-Minoan script. H 22.

Biliography: Karageorghis, *BCH* C (1976), 880, fig. 76.
Cyprus Museum, Nicosia. Kition area II/4252.

125 Ivory lion
Late Bronze Age (about 1200 BC)
Kition, Temple 4; Department of Antiquities excavations. Plaque in the form of a lion in a 'flying leap' with engraved details on both sides. Worn. L 13·3; H 3·7.
The 'flying leap' is a characteristic Mycenaean motif.
Bibliography: Karageorghis, *BCH* C (1976), 880, fig. 77.
Cyprus Museum, Nicosia. Kition area II/4242 and 4248.

126 Ivory pipe
Late Bronze Age (about 1200 BC)
Kition, Temple 4; Department of Antiquities excavations. Cylindrical pipe decorated with engraved linear designs and a Cypro-Minoan inscription.
Bibliography: Karageorghis, *BCH* C (1976), 880, fig. 78; Idem, *Antiquity* L (June 1976), 125ff.
Cyprus Museum, Nicosia. Kition area II/4267.

127 Ivory plaque with a woman
Late Bronze Age (1300–1225 BC)
Kition, Acropolis at Bamboula; French excavations. Probably from a box (pyxis). Decorated in high relief on one side with a woman seated in three-quarter view to the right. Her left arm is raised and holds a mirror, her right arm rests on her knee. Her breasts are bare and she wears a long skirt. Broken down one edge. W 4·2; H 7·5.
Bibliography: Karageorghis, *BCH* CI (1977), 763.
Cyprus Museum, Nicosia. French excavations, no. 53.

128 Ivory disc
Late Bronze Age (1300–1225 BC)

Kition, Acropolis at Bamboula; French excavations. Probably the bottom of a circular box. Engraved decoration on one side showing an elaborate floral design within a border decorated with a cable pattern. Broken around edges and slit through one side. D 16.
Bibliography: Karageorghis, *BCH* CI (1977), 763, fig. 95.
Cyprus Museum, Nicosia.

129 Ivory 'purse'
Late Bronze Age (1300–1225 BC)
Kition; Department of Antiquities excavations. In the form of a stylised flower with two groups of deeply incised horizontal flutes on the front. L 5·6; W 5·6.
Bibliography: Buchholz and Karageorghis (1973), 163, no. 1745.
Cyprus Museum, Nicosia. Kition area I/260.

130 Mycenaean terracotta figurine, the 'psi' type
Late Bronze Age (1300–1225 BC)
Kition, Temenos A; Department of Antiquities excavations. In the form of the Greek letter ψ (psi) as no. 111. Decoration in red glossy paint indicating facial features. The dress is decorated with groups of oblique lines over the breast and arms and broad vertical stripes on lowest part of body. H 10·8.
Bibliography: Karageorghis, *BCH* XCVII (1973), 651, fig. 82.
Cyprus Museum, Nicosia. Kition area II/3219.

131 Steatite vessel (amphoriskos)
Late Bronze Age (1200–1125 BC)
Probably from Kition; purchased.
Ovoid vessel with cylindrical neck surrounded below by a fillet, and conical foot. Bull's head in relief on either side of the shoulder; lower part of body decorated with leaves in relief like the calyx of a flower. H 11·7.
Bibliography: Dikaios, *RDAC* (1937–9), 202, pl. 42·4; Buchholz and Karageorghis (1973), 156, no. 1668.
Cyprus Museum, Nicosia. 1938/VI–23/5.

132 Animal-shaped vessel (askos), Proto-White Painted ware

Late Bronze Age (1100–1050 BC)

Kition, Tomb II; Department of Antiquities excavations.
Animal protome (forepart) at one end and spout at the other with tall basket handle between. Cylindrical body with sloping shoulder and knob on top. Body, handle and protome decorated with encircling bands; elaborate triangles on 'lid'.
L 15·3; W 13·3; H 13·2.

> *Bibliography:* Karageorghis. *BCH* C (1976), 880, fig. 80.

Cyprus Museum, Nicosia. Kition T 11/100.

133 Terracotta mask

Late Bronze Age (1100–1050 BC)

Kition, Temple 5; Department of Antiquities excavations.
A human face painted in red with black indicating the features including the hair and beard. W 14·8; H 16·5.

Other clay masks have been found in Late Bronze Age Cyprus, including one very similar to this in the Sanctuary of the 'Ingot God' at Enkomi. Like the Oxen masks (no. 254) they were evidently worn for religious ceremonies. The earliest examples came from sanctuaries and tombs in Syria where the practice continued into the Iron Age, as it does in Cyprus and Punic centres in the western Mediterranean.

> *Bibliography:* Karageorghis (1976), 102, pl. xvi.

Cyprus Museum, Nicosia. Kition area II/3809.

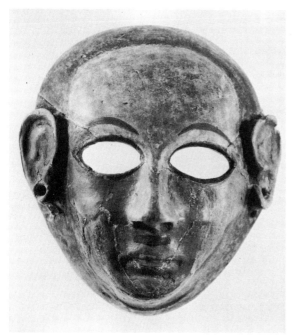

133

Palaepaphos

Under the houses of the modern village of Kouklia, near the south-eastern coast, lie the remains of ancient Paphos or Palaepaphos, the town of the mythical king Kinyras, the centre of the cult of Aphrodite in Cyprus. It was excavated by a British team in the 1950s and earlier, in 1888, the British uncovered remains of the temple of Aphrodite. Since 1966 a German/Swiss mission has been investigating several areas of the ancient town including the Temple of Aphrodite. Late Bronze Age tombs, dating from the fourteenth to the eleventh century BC, have been found at Kouklia, particularly in the localities of Evreti and Xerolimni, which yielded important ceramic finds as well as objects of bronze and gold, including rings with bezels of enamel in the cloisonné technique (no. 135). It was only recently, however, that the first Late Bronze Age architectural remains came to light at the site of the Temple of Aphrodite, demonstrating beyond doubt that this temple, thought previously to be of Roman date, was originally built about 1200 BC, at the time when the large temples of Kition were constructed. This important discovery provides archaeological evidence for the statement in Homer's Odyssey *that at Paphos Aphrodite had a temple and a fragrant altar.*

Palaepaphos is traditionally said to have been built by Agapenor, a hero of the Trojan War from Tegea, who was, according to Pausanias, the founder of the first temple of Aphrodite. [V. K.]

134 Ivory mirror handle

Late Bronze Age (1200–1125 BC)

Palaepaphos, Evreti, Tomb 8; British excavations.
Decorated in high relief on both sides with a warrior slaying a rampant lion. L 21·5.

A similar mirror handle showing a warrior slaying a griffin was found at Enkomi and is now in the British Museum (GR 1897.4–1.872).

> *Bibliography:* Catling, *BCH* XCII (1968), 168, nos. 7, 26, 34; Buchholz and Karageorghis (1973), 163, no. 1748.

Cyprus Museum, Nicosia.

with cloisons of enamel and surrounded by two rows of granulation. D 2·2.

These rings and the Kourion sceptre (no. 155) are the earliest true cloisonné enamelling known in the Mycenaean world. Although the technique of these pieces is new, the form is not, and this suggests that they were made locally either by an immigrant craftsman or by a Cypriot who had learnt the technique elsewhere, possibly in Egypt.

Bibliography: Higgins (1961), 24ff; Catling, *BCH* XCII (1968), 168, fig. 2; Buchholz and Karageorghis (1973), 167, nos. 1785–1787.

Cyprus Museum, Nicosia.

136 Pair of gold earrings

Late Bronze Age (1200–1150 BC)

Palaepaphos, Evreti, Tomb 8; British excavations.

Hoops of thin wire threaded with bulls' heads stamped from sheet gold. L 3.

Compare the pair from Kition no. 117.

Bibliography: Catling, *BCH* XCII (1968), 168, fig. 2.

137 Ten gold earrings

Late Bronze Age (1200–1150 BC)

Palaepaphos, Evreti,, Tomb 8; British excavations.

Leech-shaped; solid with overlapping ends. L 4.

This elongated version of the tapered hoop is common in twelfth-century Cyprus and may be adapted from a Syrian type.

Bibliography: Catling, *BCH* XCII (1968), 168, fig. 2.

Cyprus Museum, Nicosia.

138 Pair of gold bracelets

Late Bronze Age (1200–1150 BC)

Palaepaphos, Evreti, Tomb 8; British excavations.

Each composed of two bands of gold ribbed on the outside. D 8·7.

134

138

135 Six gold finger-rings with enamel decoration

Late Bronze Age (1200–1150 BC)

Palaepaphos, Evreti, Tomb 8; British excavations.

Broad hoop, bordered by twisted wire and decorated on the outside with impressed flame designs. Circular bezels filled

Bibliography: Catling, *BCH* XCII (1968), 168, fig. 2.

Cyprus Museum, Nicosia.

139 Wide two-handled bowl (kalathos), Proto-Bichrome ware
Late Bronze Age (1100–1050 BC)
Palaepaphos, Xerolimni, tomb 9; Department of Antiquities excavations.
Decorated in black and dark red or orange matt paint. The field in the handle zone is divided into panels filled with geometric and figured designs including a lyre player, figures with raised arms, a goat, birds and a palm tree; below, encircling bands and cross-hatched lozenges. Broken and mended. H 15; D 17.
  Bibliography: Karageorghis, *RDAC* (1967), 5, 17f., no. 7, pl. 1; Buchholz and Karageorghis (1973), 154, no. 1651; Karageorghis and des Gagniers (1974), Texte 5, no. A1, pl. 1ff.
  Cyprus Museum, Nicosia.

140 Ring vase, Proto-White Painted ware
Late Bronze Age (1100–1050 BC)
Palaepaphos, Xerolimni, Tomb 9; Department of Antiquities excavations.
Decorated in orange to black matt paint; double triangles around ring on both sides, encircling bands on neck, broad bands around rim and on handles. H 17; D 11.
  Bibliography: Karageorghis, *RDAC* (1967), 6f., 20, no. 19, fig, 9, pl. 2.
  Cyprus Museum, Nicosia.

141 Horn-shaped bottle, Proto-White Painted ware
Late Bronze Age (1100–1050 BC)
Palaepaphos, Xerolimni, Tomb 9.
Funnel mouth and two lug handles on the back. Decorated in orange to dark brown matt paint; oblique zones on body filled with lozenges, zig-zags and triangles. L 18·5; D (mouth) 4·3.
  Bibliography: Karageorghis, *RDAC* (1967), 7, 20f., no. 21, fig. 9, pl. 3; Buchholz and Karageorghis (1933), 154, no. 1656.
  Kouklia Museum.

142 Bird-shaped vessel (askos), Proto-Bichrome ware
Late Bronze Age (1100–1050 BC)
Palaepaphos, Tomb 9; Department of Antiquities excavations.
Outstretched wings and conical base with a basket handle and spout on the back. Decorated in matt black and purple. Horizontal zones filled with latticed lozenges and hatched triangles on body; broad and narrow bands elsewhere; eyes painted. L 20; H 14.
  Bibliography: Karageorghis, *RDAC* (1967), 8f., 22, no. 39, fig. 10, pl. 3.
  Cyprus Museum, Nicosia.

142

143 Inscribed gold finger-ring
Late Bronze Age (1200–1150 BC)
Palaepaphos, Evreti, Tomb 8; British excavations.
Lapis lazuli setting; on the bezel two recumbent bulls, one to the left in profile; the second, in the foreground to the right, its head turned to the spectator. Above, two script signs. D 2·2.
  Bibliography: Kenna, *BCH* XCII (1968), 157ff.; Catling, *Ibid.*, 166, no. 28.
  Cyprus Museum, Nicosia.

Writing

The earilest evidence for writing in Cyprus comes from Late Bronze Age Enkomi, where a fragmentary baked clay tablet with engraved signs in what is known as the Cypro-Minoan script was found in a layer dated about 1500 BC. This script is akin to the Linear A script of Minoan Crete and was probably borrowed by the Cypriots who had, like the Cretans, a commercial colony at Ugarit on the Syrian coast. Otherwise one cannot explain how this script was passed to the Cypriots, who had no close and direct relations with Minoan Crete during this period.

Tablets with texts in the Cypro-Minoan script were found at Enkomi but the script was known throughout Late Bronze Age Cyprus. Unlike the Aegean tablets, the Cypriote tablets are large, with engraved signs in various columns; they were baked, following a Near Eastern tradition. The Cypro-Minoan script has not yet been deciphered, in spite of several efforts, and it is unlikely that its texts are in Greek. Unfortunately the Eteo-Cypriote language, probably the local tongue in the Late Bronze Age, remains unknown.

The script continued down to the end of the Bronze Age. It 'disappeared' during the Dark Ages but reappeared during the eighth century BC to survive down to the Hellenistic period side by side with the Greek alphabet (see p. 100 below). [V. K.]

144 Inscribed gold finger-ring
Late Bronze Age (1300–1225 BC)
Kition, Tomb 9, lower burial; Department of Antiquities excavations.
Flat hoop with elliptical bezel. On the bezel engraved decoration showing a bird with open wings and three signs in the Cypro-Minoan script within an engraved border. L (of bezel) 1·5; D (hoop) 1·9.
Bibliography: Buchholz and Karageorghis (1973), 167, no. 1782; *Kition* I, 44, 61, no. 10, pl. 66.
Cyprus Museum, Nicosia.

145 Bronze ploughshare
Late Bronze Age (1200–1150 BC)
Probably Enkomi; given by Mr Kyriakos Stylianou of Larnaca. Short socket, blade with convex sides and rounded tip bearing three impressed syllabic characters. L 24; W 7·7.

145   146

Bibliography: Karageorghis, *BCH* LXXXIII (1959), 338, fig. 2; Catling (1964), 80ff., no. 13, pl. 4e; Buchholz and Karageorghis (1973), 171, no. 1892.
Cyprus Museum, Nicosia. 1958/VI–24/10.

146 Bone stylus (writing implement)
Late Bronze Age (about 1250–1190 BC)
Enkomi.
Bottom sheared and sharpened to a point. Suspension hole through the top. L 14·5.
Cyprus Museum, Nicosia. Enkomi 4548.

147 Terracotta tablet with Cypro-Minoan inscription
Late Bronze Age (1220–1190 BC)
Enkomi; Department of Antiquities excavations.
Inscribed on both sides before firing. Fragmentary. W 9; H 10.
Bibliography: *Enkomi* I, 279, area I no. 1687, II 689, 885ff., IIIa pls. 88/48, 132/36, 190/2–3; Buchholz and Karageorghis (1973), 173, no. 1906.
Cyprus Museum, Nicosia.

147

Crudely made with facial features incised before firing; on one side four Cypro-Minoan signs engraved before firing. Horns missing, feet restored. L 12; H 8·5.

Bibliography: Karageorghis, *BCH* (1971), 350, figs. 25–26. Cyprus Museum, Nicosia. 1970/XI–30/3.

148 Clay ball, inscribed with four Cypro-Minoan signs
Late Bronze Age (1300–1225 BC)
Kition, Temple 5; Department of Antiquities excavations. D 2.
 Bibliography: Karageorghis, *BCH* C (1976), 877, fig. 72. Cyprus Museum, Nicosia. Kition area II/4215.

149 Terracotta bull with Cypro-Minoan inscription
Late Bronze Age (1200–1150 BC)
Psilatos.

149

Other Late Bronze Age Finds

150 Ivory vase (rhyton)
Late Bronze Age (1450–1225 BC)
Athienou, Bamboularin tis Koukouninas; Israeli excavations.
Small vase, fluted at the rim and decorated on the body with
four zones of floral patterns including papyrus flowers.
Broken at bottom. H 12·4; D 3·9.
  Cyprus Museum, Nicosia.

151 Glass bottle
Late Bronze Age (1400–1225 BC)
Arpera; Cyprus Museum excavations.
Slender bottle crowned by a pomegranate. L 22·2.
  The form of the pomegranate is so like that of the flasks
(as no. 97) that this piece too must be a Cypriote product.
  Bibliography: SCE IV. ID, 530, fig. 71.4; Buchholz and
Karageorghis (1973), 158, no. 1681.
  Cyprus Museum, Nicosia.

152 Faience dish, blue glaze
Late Bronze Age (1450–1225 BC)
Unknown provenance.
Painted decoration in brown-black on the inside showing the
Egyptian god 'Bes' naked and squatting. To his right two
figures, one of whom is dancing. Below a bud, a fish and
flowers. H 4·2; D 13·2.
  This belongs to the Egyptianising group of faience vessels
found in Late Bronze Age Cyprus which may be imports.
  Bibliography: Peltenburg, Πρακτικα του Πρωτου
Διεθνου Κυπρολογικου Συνεδριου Part A (1972), 131,
pl. 23.1; Buchholz and Karageorghis (1973), 157, no. 1679.
  Cyprus Museum, Nicosia. G63.

153 Faience jug, light blue glaze
Unknown provenance.
Squat spherical body on base ring. Wide cylindrical neck
with handle from below mouth to shoulder. Decorated in
black. Triangles around neck bordered by bands; frieze of
circles on shoulder. H 8·5; D (max.) 7·4; (mouth) 5.2.
  Bibliography: SCE IV. 1D, 525, fig. 70. 32; Buchholz and
Karageorghis (1973), 156, no. 1673.
  Cyprus Museum, Nicosia. 1957/III–1/8.

154 Faience sceptre head, blue glaze
From a Late Bronze Age context (1190–1175 BC)
Hala Sultan Tekke; Swedish excavations.
Lotus shaped. Decorated on the top with the cartouche of
the Egyptian Pharaoh Horemheb (1348–1320 BC). Traces of
an ivory rod. H 3·5; D 3·6.

150   151

152

154

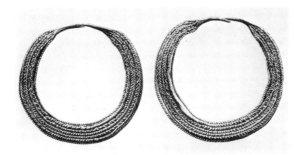

157

156

This is the only document of Horemheb yet found in Cyprus but Hala Sultan Tekke has also produced a cartouche of the Pharaoh Seti I who reigned at the end of the fourteenth century BC.

Bibliography: Karageorghis, *BCH* CII (1978), 914, fig. 79.
Cyprus Museum, Nicosia. Hala Sultan Tekke 811.

155 Gold and enamel sceptre

Late Bronze Age (1100–1050 BC)
Kourion, Kaloriziki; Tomb excavated by American team.
Tubular gold rod surmounted by a sphere bordered below by two rows of beads or granulation. On the sphere perch a pair of falcons. Both sphere and birds are decorated with cloisons outlined in gold and filled with white, green and mauve enamel. L 16·5.

Bibliography: McFadden, *AJA* LVIII (1954), 141, pl. 18.2; Buchholz and Karageorghis (1973), 167, no. 1788, col. pl. 4; Benson (1973), 50, T.40, no. 37.
Cyprus Museum, Nicosia. J 99.
Illustrated in colour.

156 Gold necklace with haematite seal

Late Bronze Age (1425–1225 BC)
Ayios Iakovos, Bronze Age sanctuary; Swedish excavations.
Necklace of fifteen gold beads, seven pomegranates and eight ribbed dates. In the centre, a Babylonian haematite cylinder seal in a gold setting. L 19·8.

Bibliography: SCE I, 357, nos. 3, 4, 27, pls. 67, 147; Buchholz and Karageorghis (1973), 166, no. 1773.
Cyprus Museum, Nicosia.

157 Pair of gold earrings

Late Bronze Age (1450–1225 BC)
Ayios Iakovos, Bronze Age sanctuary; Swedish excavations.
Crescent shaped; made of gold wire twisted as double loop-in-loop chain. D 4·7.

For the technique compare no. 113.

Bibliography: SCE I, 357, no. 5, pls. 67, 145; Pierides (1971), 20, pl. 9.9; Buchholz and Karageorghis (1973), 166, no. 1776.
Cyprus Museum, Nicosia.

158 Bronze sword

Late Bronze Age (1375–1300 BC)
Tamassos; Department of Antiquities excavations.
Narrow straight-sided blade with high midrib. Rat-tailed tang. L 35·2.

Bibliography: Karageorghis, *RDAC* (1965), 16, 26, Tomb VI, no. 20, fig. 7, pl. 4.
Cyprus Museum, Nicosia.

159 Bronze Sword

Late Bronze Age (1375–1300 BC)

Tamassos: Department of Antiquities excavations.

Narrow straight blade with high midrib. Rat-tailed tang. L 43·5.

Bibliography: Karageorghis, *RDAC* (1965), 18, 26, Tomb VI, no. 58, fig. 7, pl.4.

Cyprus Museum, Nicosia.

160 Bronze sword

Late Bronze Age (1200–1125 BC)

Unknown provenance.

Fish-tail hilt with five rivets. 'Naue II' type. L 55·5.

Swords of this type were brought to Cyprus by the Achaean settlers at the end of the thirteenth century. They were originally introduced to the Aegean from Europe probably by barbarian mercenaries hired by the Mycenaean kings.

Bibliography: Catling (1964), 113ff., no. 31, pl. 12i, j; Buchholz and Karageorghis (1973), 171, no. 1884.

Cyprus Museum, Nicosia.

162a

162b

161 Bronze spearhead

Late Bronze Age (1225–1190 BC)

Lythrankomi.

Tubular slit socket with rivet hole; leaf-shaped blade with strong midrib. L 25·7.

Bibliography: Buchholz and Karageorghis (1973), 171, no. 1886.

Cyprus Museum, Nicosia. 1966/III–11/1.

162a, b Bronze and lead weights

Late Bronze Age (1300–1200 BC)

Cast; hollow and filled with lead.

a Unknown provenance.

In the form of a reclining cow with head turned to the spectator. Four impressed lines on the side to indicate the weight. L 5·2; H 3·5.

Bibliography: Catling (1964), 251f., no. 1, pl. 44d; Buchholz and Karageorghis (1973), 163, no. 1739.

Cyprus Museum, Nicosia. C966.

b Palaepaphos, Evreti, Tomb 3.

In the form of a female head. H 3·8.

Bibliography: Maier, *RDAC* (1971), 43ff., pl. 20.3, 5, 6.

Cyprus Museum, Nicosia. T III/246.

Lead-filled weights are known in both the Near East and Egypt. Those found in Cyprus may have been imported. It seems likely that the Cypriots used them as trinkets or souvenirs rather than actual weights. An anthropomorphic weight, similar to 162b, from Ras Shamra (Ugarit), Syria, is identical in height but over 30g heavier.

163 Bronze female statuette

Late Bronze Age (1200–1100 BC)

Nicosia, Bairaktar quarter.

She is naked and stands with her hands resting on her hips, wearing a necklace and a pendant. Her hair is arranged with two plaits falling forwards on either shoulder. Right arm and feet missing. H 10·5.

Bibliography: Catling (1964), 257, no. 7, pl. 44, j; Buchholz and Karageorghis (1973), 162, no. 1734.

Cyprus Museum, Nicosia. 1936/VI–18/1.

164 Bronze torch holder

Late Bronze Age (1200–1100 BC)

Unknown provenance.

Flat wall bracket pierced at the top for suspension with deep rounded holder cast in one piece. Bull's head protome attached by three rivets over suspension hook. L (of holder) 14; W (of top) 8·6; H 30.

Bibliography: Catling (1964), 162, no. 1, pl. 25 b–c; Buchholz and Karageorghis (1973), 170, no. 1857.

Cyprus Museum, Nicosia.

163

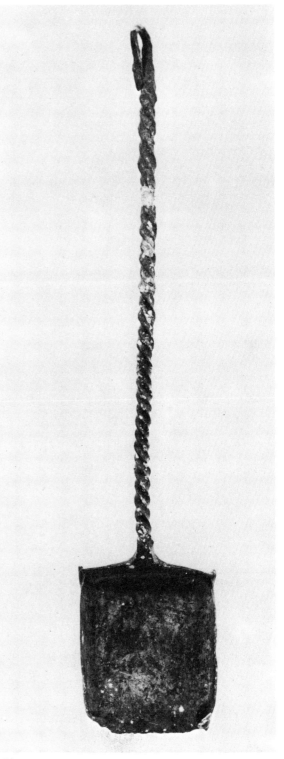

165 Bronze tongs
Late Bronze Age (1200–1100 BC)
Unknown provenance.
Cast in one piece except for the collar, which is made of twisted wire wound around near the top of the blades. L 32.5.
   These are evidently the tools of a bronzesmith and the type probably reached Cyprus from the Near East.
   Bibliography: Karageorghis, *BCH* XCIV (1970), 201ff., fig. 16.
   Cyprus Museum, Nicosia. 1969/VI-9/2.

166 Bronze charcoal shovel
Late Bronze Age (1200–1175BC)
Hala Sultan Tekke; Swedish excavations.
Handle twisted and ending in a loop for suspension. L 36·5.
   Bibliography: Karageorghis, *BCH* CI (1977), 753, fig. 80.
   Cyprus Museum, Nicosia.

166

167 Bronze tripod

Late Bronze Age (1190–1050 BC)
Episkopi, Kaloriziki, Tomb 40.
Rod type. Ring with three bead mouldings, the lower two perhaps cast in one piece. Rounded legs modelled as hooves each in one piece with a volute moulding at the top and a bull's head in the centre, joined together by struts. H 39·5; D 26·5.

Tripods and stands, used for supporting vessels such as bowls and cauldrons, are among the bronzes produced in Cyprus from the twelfth century BC. Some of the stands are decorated in the *ajouré* technique and the designs show the characteristic mixture of Aegean and Near Eastern elements. They must have been made in Cyprus where, at this time, the craftsmen could absorb Aegean and Levantine technical skills and forms.

Bibliography: Catling (1964), 194f., no. 8, pl. 28 c–e; Buchholz and Karageorghis (1973), 154, no. 1687; Benson (1973), 50, no. 39.

Cyprus Museum, Nicosia. L 299.

168 Bronze tripod

Late Bronze Age (about 1200 BC)
Unknown provenance.
Rod type similar to no. 167. Composite ring, the upper and lower bands joined by volutes and spirals made of coiled wires. Legs in two pieces brazed together; their tops are coiled with volutes and the feet hammered to look like hooves. Spirals of coiled wire between outer struts where there are usually pendant rings, possibly a sign that this is an early piece. H 11·5; D (of ring) 10·4.

Bibliography: Catling (1964), 193, pl. 27.b.

Cyprus Museum, Nicosia. L 309.

169 Bronze cauldron

Late Bronze Age (1200–1100 BC)
Paphos district, possibly Palaepaphos; purchased.
Vessel of beaten bronze with deep hemispherical body, carinated shoulder, out-turned rim and round base. Pair of double handles attached by rivets at rim and shoulder. Disc-shaped solid lid with circular boss in centre and looped handle. H (max) 59·0; D (cauldron) 59·5, lid) 4·45; Th (lid) 0·2.

This may have been found with a bronze bucket (situla) (1973/VIII–7/2) but, unlike that, it has parallels in the Aegean, including a complete example without a lid from Tiryns on the Greek mainland. Elsewhere, including at Enkomi, handles have been found. It seems likely therefore that this cauldron was made under Aegean influence, if not by an immigrant craftsman.

Bibliography: Karageorghis, *RDAC* (1974), 60ff., fig. 1, pl. 11.1–2; *Idem, BCH* XCVIII (1974), 830ff., fig. 12.

Cyprus Museum, Nicosia. 1973/VIII–71.

170 Terracotta female figurine

Late Bronze Age (1450–1225 BC)
Unknown provenance.
Naked with bird-like head, modelled eyes and nose, and ears pierced twice for large earrings. She stands with her arms bent over her breasts holding a child in her left hand. Incised lines on neck and for pubic triangle. One earring missing. H 14.

Bibliography: Karageorghis, *BCH* LXXXIX (1965), 244, fig. 19; Buchholz and Karageorghis (1973), 162, no. 1723.

Cyprus Museum, Nicosia. 1964/IX–818.

Illustrated in colour.

171 Terracotta female figurine

Late Bronze Age (1450–1225 BC)
Katydata, Tomb 28.
Flat-topped head, modelled eyes, nose and breasts. Seated on a chair shown as simply two vertical supports with her arms bent and held below her breasts and her legs stretched out before her. Incised lines below waist and indicating pubic triangle. Bands of dark purple paint below waist and around neck. H 9·5.

Bibliography: *SCE* IV.1D, 514, type II.4, fig. 70.5; Buchholz and Karageorghis (1973), 162, no. 1727.

Cyprus Museum, Nicosia. A39.

172 Terracotta boat

Late Bronze Age (1450–1225 BC)
Kazaphani, Tomb 2b, no. 249 and 377; Department of Antiquities excavations.
Attachment for mast in the centre; holes around the top of the sides for rigging. Broken and mended. L 45; H (max.) 23, W (max.) 20·5.

169

171

173

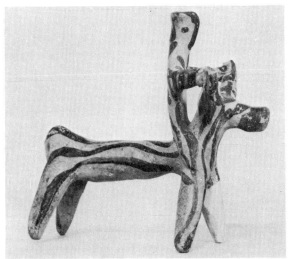

174

An interesting and unusual find, perhaps from a sailor's tomb.

Bibliography: Karageorghis, *BCH* LXXXVIII (1964), 336, fig. 70a–b; Buchholz and Karageorghis (1973), 161, no. 1719.

Cyprus Museum, Nicosia.

173 Vase in the form of a bull, Base Ring ware
Late Bronze Age (1450–1225 BC)
Unknown provenance.
Handle on the back of the neck. Incised decoration indicating eyes and forming patterns over the brow and head. Bands in matt white paint on the neck, forelegs and horns. Partly restored. L 24; H 19·2.

Cyprus Museum, Nicosia. 1974/IV–27/4.

174 Mycenaean terracotta bull and rider
Late Bronze Age (1450–1225 BC)
Unknown provenance.
The man sits forward on the bull's back and grips the horns. Painted bands all over the body of the bull and the man and some facial features painted. L 11; H 10.

Bibliography: Buchholz and Karageorghis (1973), 162, no. 1730.

Cyprus Museum, Nicosia. A32.

175 Mycenaean terracotta dog
Late Bronze Age (1450–1225 BC)
Unknown provenance.
Long ears, outstretched legs. Painted snout, eyes and ears, stripes over body. L 13; H 9·8.

Cyprus Museum, Nicosia. A35.

176 Horse-shaped vase, Proto-White Painted ware
Late Bronze Age (1100–1050 BC)
Lapithos, Tomb P. 74; Department of Antiquities excavations. Cylindrical body on low legs. Spout and basket handle on back. Decorated with dark brown to orange matt paint. Frieze of cross-hatched lozenges on body and hatched triangles on back. Bands on handle, spout and round head. Solid paint down legs and front of body showing a circle enclosing an 8-pointed star on the chest. Partly broken. L 22·7; H 25·4.
Bibliography: Pieridou, *RDAC* (1965), 88, 106, no. 122, pl. 10.
Cyprus Museum, Nicosia.

177 Ring-vase (kernos), Proto-White Painted ware
Late Bronze Age (1075–1050 BC)
Idalion, Ayios Georghios, Tomb 2; Department of Antiquities excavations.
Ring with bar across the centre supporting a basket handle. Ornament at either end of bar on ring; a miniature amphora at one end and a bull's head at the other. Decorated in matt black. Bull's features indicated. Frieze of chevrons on ring and in handle zone of amphora. H 8·3; D 19·7.
A ritual vessel.
Bibliography: Karageorghis (1965), 186, 196, no. 1, fig. 46.1, pl. 14.1–2; Buchholz and Karageorghis (1973), 154, no. 1653.
Cyprus Museum, Nicosia.

Alaas

This cemetery, on the east coast near the village of Gastria at the south end of the Karpas peninsula, was excavated by the Department of Antiquities of Cyprus in 1973 and 1974, but a number of the tombs had been looted and the objects reached private collections. However, through careful investigation, other pottery and jewellery came to light and some of the more interesting pieces here illustrate Cypriote civilisation at the close of the Late Bronze Age (1075–1050 BC). [V. A. T.-B.]

178 Bottle, Proto-White Painted ware
Late Bronze Age (1125–1050 BC)
Alaas, Tomb 16; Department of Antiquities excavations.
Tall cylindrical body, narrow neck and handle from centre of the neck to shoulder. Cross-hatched triangles on shoulder. Vertical cross-hatched panels and a panel of cross hatched lozenges with wide bands around body. Solid paint on neck and foot. H 23·5.
Bibliography: Karageorghis (1975), 14, no. 14, pls. 10, 56.
Cyprus Museum, Nicosia.

179 Bird-shaped bottle (askos), Proto-White Painted ware
Late Bronze Age (1125–1050 BC)
Alaas, Tomb 16; Department of Antiquities excavations.
Stands on three small feet. Pinched rim and basket handle. Decorated with ovals on either side of body and bands on neck and handle. L 10; H 7.
Bibliography: Karageorghis (1975), 15, no. 18, pls. 10, 58.
Cyprus Museum, Nicosia.

180 Pair of gold earrings
Late Bronze Age (1125–1050 BC)
Alaas, Tomb 16; Department of Antiquities excavations.
Plain gold wire forming a tapered hoop with ends overlapping and twisted around each other. D 1·7.

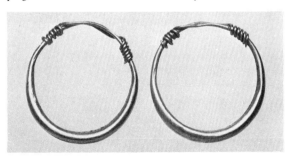

180

These earrings are popular in Cyprus from about 1400 BC and were probably adopted from the East, although examples have also been found in Crete. They survive in Cyprus through the Geometric period and are re-introduced to Greece in the seventh century BC.

Bibliography: Karageorghis (1975), 15, nos. 20–21, pls. 8, 58.

Cyprus Museum, Nicosia.

181 'Pilgrim' flask, Proto-White Painted ware
Late Bronze Age (1125–1050 BC)
Alaas, Tomb 16; Department of Antiquities excavations.
Decorated on one side with a solid six-pointed star in a circle and on the other with a smaller star within a circle bordered by triangles. Bands on neck and handles. H 16.

Bibliography: Karageorghis (1975), 15, no. 23, pls. 11, 57.
Cyprus Museum, Nicosia.

181

182 Bird-shaped vessel (askos), Proto-White Painted ware
Late Bronze Age (1125–1050 BC)
Alaas, Tomb 17; Department of Antiquities excavations.

Standing on three short feet with basket handle and spout on the back. Body decorated with cross-hatched triangles; chevrons on neck. L 15; H 10·2.

Bibliography: Karageorghis (1975), 17f., no. 11, pls. 13, 60.
Cyprus Museum, Nicosia.

183 Vessel (hydria), Proto-White Painted ware
Late Bronze Age (1125–1050 BC)
Alaas, Tomb 19; Department of Antiquities excavations.
Decorated with wavy bands in handle frieze and cross-hatched lozenges on shoulder. Broad and narrow bands on neck and rest of body. H 40.

Bibliography: Karageorghis (1975), 21, no. 2, pls. 17, 62.
Cyprus Museum, Nicosia.

184 Vessel (stirrup jar), Proto-Bichrome ware
Late Bronze Age (1125–1050 BC)
Alaas, Tomb 19; Department of Antiquities excavations.
Decorated in black and purple. Geometric patterns on shoulder, a frieze of lozenges below and bands encircling body. H 40.

Bibliography: Karageorghis (1975), 22, no. 13, pls. 18, 63.
Cyprus Museum, Nicosia.

Limassol

185 Terracotta quadruped
Late Bronze Age/early Geometric period (1100–1000 BC)
Limassol, Komissariato quarter, sanctuary site, found with nos. 186 and 197.
Cylindrical, wheel-made body, short legs, pointed ears. L 17·3; H 12·3.

Animal figures of this type were regularly offered in Minoan sanctuaries from the earlier second millennium and, like the goddess with uplifted arms, they were probably adopted from Crete (see also nos. 186, 187).

Bibliography: Karageorghis, *BCH* CI (1977), 720, fig. 30. Limassol Museum. 580/5.

186 Terracotta goddess with uplifted arms, White Painted ware
Late Bronze Age/early Geometric period (1100–1000 BC)
Limassol, found with nos. 185 and 187.
Bell-shaped wheel-made body decorated with groups of encircling bands and triangles. Pellets for eyes and breasts, modelled nose. Broken and mended, partly restored. H 23·7.

Bibliography: Karageorghis, *BCH* CI (1977), 719f., fig. 28. Limassol Museum. 580/7.

187 Terracotta goddess with uplifted arms, White Painted ware
Late Bronze Age/early Geometric period (1100–1000 BC)
Limassol, found with nos. 185, 186.
As no. 186. H 23·7.

Bibliography: Karageorghis, *BCH* CI (1977), 729f., fig. 27. Limassol Museum. 580/8.

The Geometric Period

The beginning of the Iron Age in Cyprus is traditionally placed in the mid-eleventh century BC. No great event marks the change, and indeed by this time iron had already been in use for a century. The first two hundred years are a 'dark age' marked by depopulation and a general decline in standards of living. Most of our information of the early period comes from cemeteries but some new sites were founded often in the same place as or in the neighbourhood of their Bronze Age predecessors (see also p. 37 f. above). Contacts were maintained to a certain extent with the Near East and the Aegean, in particular with Crete. Some pottery was imported and its shapes and decoration imitated. Terracottas and jewellery in general continue in the forms established in the preceding era, some types being later reintroduced to the Greek world from Cyprus (e.g. no. 180).

The mid-ninth century saw a revival of Cypriote culture and an increase in population. The Phoenicians may have been partly responsible. The date of their colonisation of Cyprus is still uncertain but they were certainly established at Kition, which was now reoccupied for the first time for 150 years (see p. 83 below). Typical Phoenician Red Slip and Black-on-Red pottery had been imported earlier but from about 850 BC it is locally made either in Phoenician shapes, which are in turn copied by the Cypriots in their own White Painted and Bichrome fabrics, or in shapes already current in their repertoire. The vase shapes are in general more articulate. The ornaments are more carefully drawn and we see the pictorial style (see nos. 212–214 below) in its early stages. By the end of the period the Cypriots were literate again (no. 314 below) and by the mid-eighth century the first monumental tombs at Salamis were under construction and we are looking forward to the *floruit* of the Cypro-Archaic period. [V. A. T.-B.]

188, 189 Terracotta vessels (naiskoi), White Painted ware
Geometric period (1050–1000 BC)
Kition, a) outside Temple 1; b) outside Temple 5; Department of Antiquities excavations.

188

191

Both are models of sanctuaries each with three window-like openings standing on a conical base. Considerably restored. **188** Decorated with bands and linear designs around body and openings; triangles on shoulder. H 16; D (max) 12·5.

Bibliography: Karageorghis, *BCH* XCIV (1970), 28ff., fig. 1; *idem* (1976), 91, pl. 66.

Cyprus Museum, Nicosia. Kition, area II/1776.

189 Decorated simply with encircling bands. H 13·5; D (max) 9·3.

Bibliography: Karageorghis, *BCH* C (1976), 879.

Cyprus Museum, Nicosia. Kition, area II/1778.

Examples from Crete date from the third millennium and a number are contemporary with these Cypriote pieces. They are therefore further evidence for the strong ties between Crete and Cyprus in the eleventh century BC.

190 Multiple vessel, White Painted ware

Geometric period (1050–950 BC)

Kition, Tomb 11; Department of Antiquities excavations.

Composed of seven gourd-shaped vessels joined together, star-shaped pattern on body at either end. Diagonal or horizontal bands on handles. Hatched triangles or lozenges encircling sides. Partly restored. L 25·2; H 15·1; D 10·6–11·8.

Bibliography: Karageorghis, *BCH* C (1976), 880, fig. 81.

Cyprus Museum, Nicosia.

191 Terracotta mask from a vase

Geometric period (1050–1000 BC)

Kition, near temple 5; Department of Antiquities excavations.

Bearded male head wearing a kind of crown; eyes hollowed; moulded. W 9·8; H 11·7.

One of two originally attached to a cylindrical vase. The Cypriots do not in general use the mould for terracotta figurines until the later eighth century. However the technique has a long history in the East and appears in Syria in the mid-second millennium. At present this is a sporadic early occurrence in Cyprus.

Bibliography: Karageorghis, *BCH* C (1976), 879, fig. 75.

Cyprus Museum, Nicosia. Kition, area II/4083.

192 Terracotta goddess with uplifted arms

Geometric period (1050–1000 BC)

Kition, deposit outside Temple I; Department of Antiquities excavations.

Hand-made trumpet-shaped body. Modelled breasts and nose. She wears a low head-dress; a painted band around the neck indicates the neckline. Left arm broken and part of head missing H 10·9.

Bibliography: Cf. Karageorghis (1976), 91, pl. 66.

Cyprus Museum, Nicosia. Kition, area II/2340.

193 Terracotta goddess with uplifted arms
Geometric period (1050–950 BC)
Morphou, Toumba tou Skourou.
Hand-made hollow trumpet-shaped body, modelled ears,
nose and breasts. Brown painted bands around neck, arms,
wrists and body forming a check pattern for the skirt. H 16.
 Bibliography: BCH LXXXIII (1959), 339, fig. 4.
 Cyprus Museum, Nicosia. 1958/V–7/3.
 Illustrated in colour.

194 Terracotta horse and rider
Geometric period (1050–950 BC)
Unknown provenance.
Hand-made. Decorated with linear ornaments in black matt
paint; eyes indicated. L 14·5; H 13·6.
 Bibliography: Karageorghis, *BCH* XCVIII (1974), 833ff.,
fig. 14.
 Cyprus Museum, Nicosia. 1973/XI–14/1.

195 Jar, White Painted ware
Geometric period (1050–950 BC)
From Kourion.
Large vessel with conical foot and pair of strap handles on
shoulder. Decorated on body in panels. The central metope
(panel) on one side shows an elaborate geometric pattern
with, to the left, a bird and a serpent. The central metope on
the other side shows a large comb motif with a swastika and a
wheel. The metopes are bordered by horizontal and vertical
zones filled with geometric patterns. Frieze of triangles
filled with cross-hatched lozenges on shoulder. Bands around
rim, below main friezes and on handles. H 35; D (max) 31·2.

195

Bibliography: Karageorghis and des Gagniers (1974),
Texte 60, no. XXII·1, pl. 218f.
 Cyprus Museum, Nicosia. B63.

196 Bowl, White Painted ware
Geometric period (1050–950 BC)
Lapithos, Ayia Anastasia, Tomb 2; Cyprus Museum
excavations 1915.
Deep bowl with two loop handles on conical foot; panel
decoration on body in matt black showing elaborate geo-

194

196

metric motifs and in centre a tree on which perch two birds.
Broad and narrow bands on lower part of body and foot.
H 14; D 18·5.

Bibliography: Pieridou, *RDAC* (1966), 4, no. 29, pl. 3·7–8;
Karageorghis and des Gagniers (1974), Texte 67, no.
XXVe·1, pl. 356.

Cyprus Museum, Nicosia.

197 Ring vase (kernos), White Painted ware
Geometric period (1050–950 BC)
Rizokarpaso, Anavrysi, Tomb 1; bought from Maria Dimitri.
Four vessels (amphorae) and two animal heads set on a large
ring. The animal heads, joined by a basket handle, are a bull
and a Cypriote goat. Of the amphorae two have vertical
handles and two loop handles. Purple-black decoration of
bands and circles around ring and amphorae and indicating
features on the animal heads. H 19·8; D 30.

Bibliography: du Plat Taylor, *RDAC* (1937–9), 15 no. 34,
pl. 14·1.

Cyprus Museum, Nicosia. 1937/V-1/3.

197

199

198 Gold pendant
Geometric period (1050–950 BC)
Unknown provenance.
Disc with conical projection in the centre. Filigree decoration
bordering disc and projection. A hollow ribbed cylinder
serves as the suspension ring. D 3·3.

Bibliography: Pierides (1971), 24, pl. 13·4.

Cyprus Museum, Nicosia. J506.

199 Terracotta warrior
Geometric period (950–900 BC)
Rizokarpaso, Latsia; Department of Antiquities excavations.
Bell-shaped body with two holes for detachable legs on the
lower part. Crested helmet perforated on top. Eyes and
mouth painted in matt black and black bands around body
and on helmet. End of left arm missing. H 11·7.

Similar figures have been found in Attic tombs, also of the
later tenth century. Found with nos. 200, 201.

Bibliography: Christou, *RDAC* (1972), 151, 154, no. 45,
pl. 26.

Cyprus Museum, Nicosia. CS 1817/45

200 Terracotta bird
Geometric period (950–900 BC)
Rizokarpaso, Latsia; Department of Antiquities excavations.
Wheel-made. Long neck, open wings and fan-shaped tail.
Stands on a tall conical base. Linear decoration in matt black
forming latticed pattern on wings and tail and chevrons on
neck. L 11·4; H 6·8.

Birds, usually identified as cocks, are found in eighth-
century tombs in the Greek world and this early example
from a known context in Cyprus adds further weight to the

suggestion that the type originated in the island. Found with nos. 199, 201.

Bibliography: Christou, *RDAC* (1972), 148, 154f., no. 16, pl. 26.

Cyprus Museum, Nicosia. CS 1817/16.

201 Pair of gold earrings

Geometric period (950–900 BC)

Rizokarpaso, Latsia; Department of Antiquities excavations.

Circular hoop; hollow with the ends turned back and twisted around to form loops. D 2·4.

Found with the terracottas, nos. 199, 200.

Bibliography: Christou *RDAC* (1972), 149, 154, nos. 24, 25, pl. 26.

Cyprus Museum, Nicosia. CS 1817/24, 25.

202 Gold mounting

Geometric period (850–750 BC)

Kythrea, Ayios Demetrianos.

Disc-shaped. Decorated in repoussé with an eight-petalled rosette. D 2.

Bibliography: Pierides (1971), 25, pl. 13·11.

Cyprus Museum, Nicosia.

203 a–c Three gold mountings

Geometric period (850–750 BC)

Lapithos, Tomb 403; Swedish excavations.

Rectangular with folded edges and holes at the upper corners for attachment.

a Decorated in repoussé with a female head, her long hair arranged so that locks fall forward onto either shoulder. She wears a necklace and a pendant. L 4·3; W 3·5.

Bibliography: SCE I, 187, no. 1, pl. 44; Pierides (1971), 23f., pl. 13·2.

b Decorated in repoussé with a frontal naked woman. She has long hair and stands with her arms bent and raised. L 4·7; W 3·5.

Bibliography: SCE I, 188, no. 40, pl. 44, 155·14; Pierides (1971), 23, pl. 13·1.

c Decorated in repoussé as the last. L 4·7; W 3·5.

Bibliography: SCE I, 189, no. 92, pl. 44; Pierides (1971), 24, pl. 13·3.

These mountings probably formed part of a Near Eastern type of head-dress known as a *polos*.

Cyprus Museum, Nicosia.

204 Pair of gold earrings

Geometric period (850–750 BC)

Lapithos, Tomb 403; Swedish excavations.

Solid hoop with overlapping ends; pendants of clusters of four balls. L 2·2.

Bibliography: SCE I, 188, nos. 36, 38, pls. 44, 155·8; Pierides (1971), 25, pl. 13·10.

Cyprus Museum, Nicosia.

205 Gold earring

Geometric period (850–750 BC)

Amathus, Tomb 14; Swedish excavations.

Circular with overlapping ends partly elongated by pinching; a cluster of balls attached below. L 4.

Bibliography: SCE II, 85, no. 2, pls. 20, 155·31; Pierides (1971), 24, pl. 13·5.

Cyprus Museum, Nicosia.

206 Gold earring

Geometric period (850–750 BC)

Tamassos.

Circular hoop with pendant of five balls attached by gold wire twisted around the earring. Loops at end of hoop missing. L 3.

Bibliography: Pierides (1971), 24, pl. 13·6.

Cyprus Museum, Nicosia. J211.

207 Gold earring

Geometric period (850–750 BC)

Palaepaphos.

Circular with the ends bent back to form hooks. Wire wound around hook at lower end. Solid. D 3.

Bibliography: Pierides (1971), 25, pl. 13·8.

Cyprus Museum, Nicosia. J307.

208 Gold earring

Geometric period (850–750 BC)

Vatyli.

203a

204

207

208

Circular hoop; hollow with the ends turned back and twisted around to form loops. D 3.

> *Bibliography:* Pierides (1971), 24f., pl. 13·7.

Cyprus Museum, Nicosia. J212.

209 Pair of gold-plated bronze spiral finger-rings
Geometric period (850–750 BC)
Lapithos; Cyprus Archaeological survey. D (max.) 2.

> *Bibliography:* Karageorghis, *BCH* XCVIII (1974), 840, fig. 28.

Cyprus Museum, Nicosia. CS 2010/23, 22.

210 Vessel (krater), White Painted ware
Geometric period (850–750 BC)
Unknown provenance; purchased.

Deep bowl on three loop feet with four handles below the rim, two simple straps alternating with two double handles each in the form of a horned bull's head. Panel decoration in handle zone showing elaborate triangles and swastikas with, on one side, a man to the right with uplifted arms. Below one double handle, a fish in silhouette, below the other, a bird. Broad and narrow bands below figured zone; bands on feet and handles and below rim. H 36·5; D (mouth) 27·7.

> *Bibliography:* Karageorghis and des Gagniers (1974), Texte 34, no. IX·5, pl. 101.

Cyprus Museum, Nicosia. 1964/XII–19/3.

211 Vase (amphora), White Painted ware
Geometric period (850–750 BC)
Unknown provenance; formerly G. Petrakides collection, Larnaca.

In the shoulder frieze on one side is an archer running to the right shooting at a bird. Panels on the neck filled with geometric motifs bordered by encircling bands. Broad and narrow bands below figured frieze. H 64·5; D (of mouth) 3.2.

> *Bibliography:* Karageorghis and des Gagniers (1974), Texte 18, no. III·1, pl. 31.

Cyprus Museum, Nicosia. 1970/VI–24/1.

212 Vase (The 'Hubbard' Amphora), White Painted ware
Geometric period (850–750 BC)
Probably from Platani; given by Wing-Commander O'Brien Hubbard.

In the handle zone a figured frieze showing a woman seated to the left drinking from a vase through a long straw (compare no. 214). She is approached by a female servant. Behind her, a sphinx sniffing a flower, and from the other handle springs a bull's protome (forepart). On the other side are male and female dancers holding hands, one with a lyre. Panel decoration of geometric motifs on the neck. Triangles and swastikas on the shoulders. Bands encircle body and neck above and below decoration. H 68; D (mouth) 38·5.

212

213

Bibliography: Dikaios, *BSA* XXXVII (1936–7), 56ff., pls. 7–8; Karageorghis and des Gagniers (1974), Texte 8f., pl. 6ff.

Cyprus Museum, Nicosia. 1938/XI–2/3.

213 Vase (amphora), White Painted ware
Geometric period (850–750 BC)

Khrysochou; purchased.

Handles from rim to shoulder. Figured scene on neck on either side showing two warriors in a horse-drawn cart; on one side they are led by a horseman with a bird above; on the other side the horseman appears to ride two animals and a dog moves to the left below. Groups of bands encircle the body of the vase and border the figured scene. Stripes on handle and band around rim. Repaired and partly restored. H 59; D (mouth) 36.

Bibliography: Karageorghis, *RDAC* (1973), 167ff., pls. 15–16, figs. 3–4.

Cyprus Museum, Nicosia. 1973/III–16/2.

214 Jug, Black-on-Red ware
Geometric period (850–750 BC)

Khrysochou; purchased.

Globular body, narrow cylindrical neck with handle-ridge from which springs a double handle to the shoulder. Bands encircling plain rim, on handle and upper shoulder. Below, a figured scene: a pair of confronting sphinxes either side of a tree; to the right a man seated on a high-backed chair drinks through a long straw from one of two vases on the table before him (compare no. 212); behind, walking to the left, a man holding out a flower and a fish; to the right, a bull attacked by a lion with its head turned back. H 18·5.

Bibliography: Karageorghis, *RDAC* (1974), 67ff., figs. 5–6, pls. 13–14.

Cyprus Museum, Nicosia. 1973/XII–7/1.

215 Jug, Bichrome ware
Geometric period (850–750 BC)

Unknown provenance.

Decorated in purple-red and black. On the body, fish swimming to the right with a swastika above on each side. Bands encircling neck with an 'eye' on either side below the rim. H 18.

Bibliography: Karageorghis and des Gagniers (1974), Texte 62, no. XXIVa.5, pl. 231.

Cyprus Museum, Nicosia. B801.

216 Vessel in the form of a bird (askos), Bichrome ware
Geometric period (850–750 BC)

Unknown provenance; formerly Michaelides collection.

Head, tail and wings modelled. Stands on three short feet. Spout and basket handle on back. Decorated in purple and

216

black with a frieze of cross-hatched lozenges on body and bands around neck, on beak, tail, wings, handle and spout. Eyes indicated. L 27; H 12·5.

Bibliography: Pieridou, *RDAC* (1970), 100, no. 8, pl. 16.8.

Cyprus Museum, Nicosia. 1968/V–30/321.

The Archaic Period

In the eighth century Cyprus was a prosperous land trading both with the East and with Greece. The beginning of the Archaic period in about 750 BC coincides with the increasing aggression shown by Assyria. Under Tiglath-Pileser III and his successor Sargon II Assyria extended its influence in Palestine, Syria and Phoenicia, and eventually reduced Cyprus to submission in 709 BC. Assyria, therefore, became the first of a number of foreign powers to control the island in the Iron Age. Seven Cypriote kings are recorded as paying homage to Sargon II, and in later Assyrian records we read of ten Cypriote kingdoms. Assyrian domination lasted for about fifty years. After the Assyrian Empire broke up at the end of the seventh century Egypt emerged as the major power. In about 569 BC the Pharaoh Amasis took political control of Cyprus and so brought to an end eighty glorious years of independence. Egyptian domination, however, was not to last for long as in 545 BC the Cypriote kings voluntarily surrendered to a new overlord, Persia. This was another turning point in Cypriote history. At first the island retained a considerable degree of independence, although it was included in the fifth satrapy of the Persian Empire in 521 BC, but it later shared the same fate as the East Greek cities of Ionia. Freedom of movement within the Persian Empire intensified contact between Cyprus and Ionia, and we find Cypriote art subjected to increasing East Greek influence. In 498 BC Cyprus took part in the Ionian revolt, an attempt to break away from Persian rule. As a result of the failure of the operations and the reduction by siege of several Cypriote cities, Persia strengthened her control, establishing pro-Persian kings on the Cypriote thrones and forcing the island to support operations against the Greeks.

The vicissitudes of Cypriote history and the island's involvement with the major powers leave their mark on Cypriote civilisation. Finds of the later eighth century are similar to items taken by Sargon II as booty from Nimrud (e.g. the ivories from Salamis, nos. 227–228).

There is some evidence that the island was not unified in the Geometric period, and by the Archaic period we see the rise of the city kingdoms. Regional styles of pottery and sculpture can be observed together with local differences in the Cypriote syllabic script. The monumental tombs at Salamis with their rich grave goods, the multifarious finds at Phoenician Kition, the particular ties of Marion with the Greek world, all speak for a flourishing island with wide-ranging commercial connections. This is a time too when the Cypriote character and ability to fuse and transmit elements from many sources is seen at its best and most original.

[V. A. T.-B.]

Salamis

Recent excavations at the city site of Salamis carried out by a French team revealed a tomb dating from the first half of the eleventh century (p. 37 above) which suggests that the settlement here overlapped for a short time with that of neighbouring Enkomi (destroyed about 1075 BC) to which it became the successor. The best known tombs at Salamis, however, are those investigated by the Department of Antiquities of Cyprus. Two cemeteries were found situated to the west behind the city site, the most spectacular being the so-called 'Royal' necropolis. The monumental tombs here date for the most part from the eighth and seventh centuries BC and have chambers often built of well-dressed blocks with fine façades sometimes with moulded cornices and spacious dromoi *(entrance passages). Horse and chariot burials, recalling the burial customs described by Homer, were found in the* dromoi *and some also provided evidence for human sacrifice (slaves killed to serve their masters in the after-life). Though all the chambers of these 'royal' tombs had been looted, the* dromoi *produced rich gifts, such as ivory furniture (nos. 225–228), bronze cauldrons, the metallic parts of ceremonial chariots and hearses (nos. 236–240), as well as elaborately decorated horse trappings.*

The horse trappings and chariot fittings are the most spectacular bronzes yet found in Archaic Cyprus

(nos. 229–240, 244). In general they are adopted from the Near East. Items like blinkers and front bands (the latter worn on the forehead as illustrated on the terracotta horse's head, no. 273) are of North Syrian origin, but the hinged front bands (nos. 230, 231) seem to be a particularly Cypriote variety and, if these were made locally, the same workshops may have produced the other trappings. Other pieces of decorative harness can be more directly traced back to Assyria although some were borrowed by Syria and Phoenicia in the eighth century whence they may have reached Cyprus. These include side pendant ornaments like nos. 232, 233, which were attached to the harness to hang on the horse's side and peytrels with bells or tassels (e.g. no. 235)

Horse with
harness and trappings

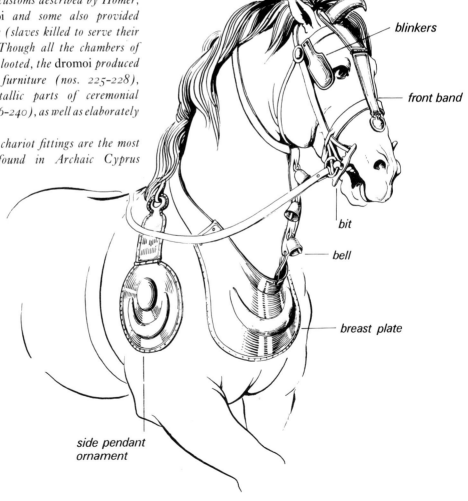

blinkers

front band

bit

bell

breast plate

*side pendant
ornament*

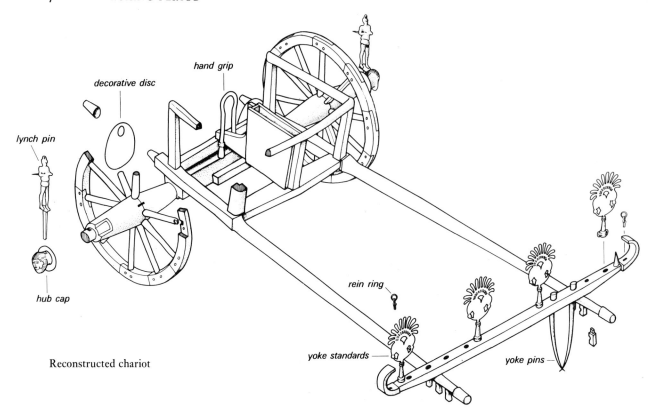

decorative disc

hand grip

lynch pin

hub cap

rein ring

yoke standards

yoke pins

Reconstructed chariot

worn around the neck. The yoke standards fixed along the yoke over the horses' necks (no. 236) are illustrated on contemporary Assyrian reliefs but some come from Zincirli in North Syria. Truly Assyrian in type are the curving breast plates (no. 234).

The cemetery at Cellarka is situated south of the 'royal' necropolis on a low ridge of hard limestone extending from north to south. This is particularly suitable for the simple rock-cut chamber tombs which were evidently for the less important sector of the population. The cemetery was in use from about 700 BC to 300 BC and the tombs served families for several generations, the earlier burials being pushed aside to make room for the later ones. Particularly interesting are the pyres in honour of the dead found in the dromoi or close to the tombs a short way below the surface and dating from the sixth to the fourth century. The ashes contained a number of offerings, all burnt, including vases evidently smashed after a libation had been offered. The practice may have been copied from Athens although there is no evidence for cremation in the Cellarka cemetery which has been associated with the Athenian pyres.

A funerary monument of the end of the fourth century BC, discovered under a tumulus on the eastern outskirts of Enkomi, proved to be the cenotaph of the last king of Salamis, Nicocreon, and the members of the royal family who committed suicide in 311 BC to avoid falling into the hands of Ptolemy of Egypt. Several clay portraits were found in the pyre of the cenotaph.

At the city site a number of monumental public buildings of the Hellenistic and Roman periods have come to light; they include a Gymnasium and a Theatre, both adorned with many marble statues.   [v. K.]

217 Gold and crystal necklace
Geometric period (775–750 BC)
Salamis, 'Royal' Tomb 1; Department of Antiquities excavations.
Six globular crystal beads with gold linings and six biconical ribbed gold beads; five additional gold cylinders originally belonging to the crystal beads now missing. L 15·5.
Bibliography: Dikaios, *AA* (1963), 147, no. 76, fig. 15; Pierides (1971), 26, pl. 14·3.
Cyprus Museum, Nicosia.

217

*218 Ivory palette
Geometric/Archaic period (about 750 BC)
Salamis, 'Royal' Tomb 1; Department of Antiquities
excavations. Rectangular, pointed at one end; engraved
decoration in panels showing crossing lines and chequer-
board pattern. L 11.
Bibliography: Dikaios, *AA* (1963), 147, no. 13, fig. 25.
Cyprus Museum, Nicosia.

219 Gold mounting
Archaic period (750–650 BC)
Salamis, 'Royal' Tomb 31; Department of Antiquities
excavations.
Elliptical with perforations at the edges; decorated in
repoussé with a two-horsed chariot (only one horse is shown)
driving to the right and a dog running below. In the car
stands the charioteer leaning forward, but only his hands
holding the reins and the lower part of his body are visible.
L 9·5; W 4·5.
Bibliography: Necropolis I, 61, 67, no. 67/2, pl. 61.
Cyprus Museum, Nicosia.

220 Jar, Bichrome ware
Archaic period (750–650 BC)
Salamis, 'Royal' Tomb 31; Department of Antiquities
excavations.

Standing on three loop legs with a pair of double handles
each forming a bull's head with eyes and outline painted.
Panel decoration on body in black and purple-red filled with
lozenges and chevrons. Encircling bands above and below.
H 13·5; D 12·5.
Bibliography: Necropolis I, 60, 65, no. 47, pls. 58, 130.
Cyprus Museum, Nicosia.

221 Feeder vase, Bichrome ware
Archaic period (750–650 BC)
Salamis, 'Royal' Tomb 31; Department of Antiquities
excavations.
Bird-shaped with pinched mouth for the head. Handle from
back of neck to shoulder. Red and black parallel bands on
body around rim and on handle. L 18; H 8.
Bibliography: Necropolis I, 59, no. 34, pls. 59, 131.
Cyprus Museum, Nicosia.

222 a, b Two ivory blinkers
Archaic period (725–650 BC)
Salamis, 'Royal' Tomb 47; Department of Antiquities
excavations.
Decorated on one side in relief with three long stemmed lotus
buds. Perforations around edge. Fragmentary. Although
derived from metal prototypes ivory blinkers are impractical
and must have served a ceremonial purpose. Similar examples have been found at Nimrud.
a L 16; W 8·8.
Bibliography: Necropolis I, 83, 87f., no. 88, pls. 81, 139.
b L 15·6; W 8·8.
Bibliography: ibid., 84, 87f., no. 91, pls. 81, 139.
Cyprus Museum, Nicosia.

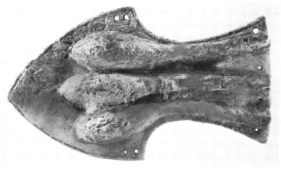

222b

223 Ivory front band
Archaic period (725–650 BC)
Salamis, 'Royal' Tomb 47; Department of Antiquities
excavations.
Rectangular terminating in a palmette. Perforations along
upper edge. L 9·2; W 6·6.

conical foot carrying two mouldings decorated with painted overhanging leaves; black and purple decoration on bowl showing vertical bands in handle zone and broader encircling bands above and below. Females painted red with black features and white eyeballs. H (stand) 27, (jar) 8·5; D (jar) 7.

Bibliography: Necropolis I, 82, 86, nos. 57 and 57a, pls. 79, 137.

Cyprus Museum, Nicosia.

223

Like the ivory blinkers, ivory front bands must have been for ceremonial use. All examples in ivory hitherto found are of this same type which follows the lower part of the metal versions. The upper part was probably of leather attached by the perforations.

Bibliography: Necropolis I, 83, 88, no. 89, pls. 81, 139.

Cyprus Museum, Nicosia.

224 Terracotta incense burner

Archaic period (725–650 BC)

Salamis, 'Royal' Tomb 47; Department of Antiquities excavations.

Deep bowl probably supported by a stand decorated in relief with a pair of female figures. They stand on a base formed by a

225

225 Ivory lamp stand

Archaic period (about 700 BC)

Salamis, 'Royal' Tomb 79; Department of Antiquities excavations.

Carved from a single piece of ivory with three series of overhanging petals on a solid stem, bearing a tripod-like support, the arms ending in volutes (compare the bronze example, no. 326). H (stem) 19·5, (whole) 30·5; D (of top disc) 8·2.

Bibliography: Necropolis III, 41, 119, no. 333, pls. F.1, 54, 236.

Cyprus Museum, Nicosia.

226 Ivory leg of a table or couch

Archaic period (about 700 BC)

Salamis, 'Royal' Tomb 79; Department of Antiquities excavations.

S-shaped ending in a lion's paw with incrusted claws resting on a semi-cylindrical base hollowed at the bottom near the socket. Attached at the top by a narrow rectangular plaque with three piercings. On the upper part a rectangular panel, now mostly missing; originally decorated with a winged sphinx inlaid in cloisonné within a beaded border. H 37; W 85; Th 7·5.

Bibliography: Necropolis III, 36, no. 249, pls. F.2, 55, 242.

Cyprus Museum, Nicosia.

227 Open-work cloisonné ivory plaque

Archaic period (about 700 BC)

Salamis, 'Royal' Tomb 79; Department of Antiquities excavations.

Shows an elaborate floral design, a 'Tree of Life'; cloisons filled with blue and red frit with gold leaf (traces of which survive) on the border. Probably originally from the arms of the throne found in this tomb. W 10·4; H 16·4; Th 0·8.

Bibliography: Necropolis III, 20, 87f., no. 143, pls. B.3–4, 62, 63, 241.

Cyprus Museum, Nicosia.

Illustrated in colour.

228 Open-work cloisonné ivory plaque

Archaic period (about 700 BC)

Salamis, 'Royal' Tomb 79; Department of Antiquities excavations.

Showing a winged sphinx walking amongst flowers. The sphinx wears an Egyptian double crown and a long apron. There is a vraeus (sacred cobra) on the forehead. Cloisons filled with blue and brownish-red paint and the borders overlaid with gold; eyes originally inlaid either with glass or ivory. Probably originally on the arms of the throne as no. 227. W 11; H 10; Th 0·5, maximum 1·2.

Bibliography: Necropolis III, 37, 87f., no. 258, pls. B.1–2, 62, 241.

Cyprus Museum, Nicosia.

Illustrated in colour.

229 Two bronze blinkers

Archaic period (about 700 BC)

Salamis, 'Royal' Tomb 79; Department of Antiquities excavations.

Sole-shaped with three pairs of perforations round the edge. Decorated in repoussé with a lion attacking a bull. Corroded. L (both) 22; W (both) 10·2.

Bibliography: Necropolis III, 24f., 81, nos. 183, 196, pls. 85, 86, 267.

Cyprus Museum, Nicosia.

229

230 Bronze front band

Archaic period (about 700 BC)

Salamis, 'Royal' Tomb 79; Department of Antiquities excavations.

Two hinged bronze plates with a curving crest. Loop at top for attachment terminating in a palmette. Decorated in high repoussé showing, on the upper plate, three couchant lions with four snakes (uraei) below. On the lower plate three naked females, their hands on their breasts, stand on lotus flowers. On their heads stand three more naked females with their arms by their sides below a winged sun disc. L 50; W (max) 11·0.

Bibliography: Necropolis III, 24, 81f., no. 190, pls. 83, 270.

Cyprus Museum, Nicosia.

231 Bronze front band

Archaic period (about 700 BC)

Salamis, 'Royal' Tomb 79; Department of Antiquities excavations.

Two bronze plates hinged together, the lower one terminating in a voluted palmette. Decorated in repoussé with figures of the god El to the left, the lower one standing below a

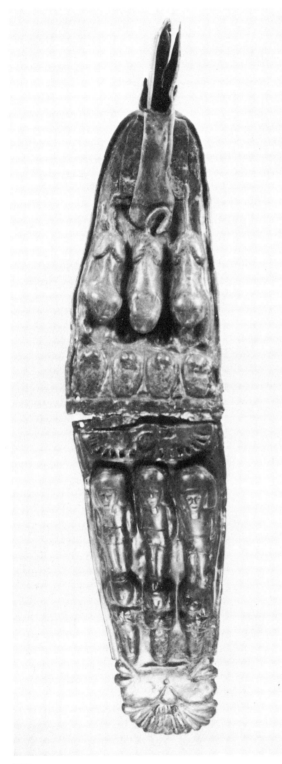

winged sun disc with a frieze of lotus flowers and buds below.
L 47·5; W 10·6.

> *Bibliography: Necropolis* III, 28, 77, no. 215, pls. 117, 269.
> Cyprus Museum, Nicosia.

232 Bronze side pendant ornament

Archaic period (about 700 BC)

Salamis, 'Royal' Tomb 79; Department of Antiquities
excavations.

Two hinged components; a rectangular plate with a rounded
top perforated for suspension and a disc. Repoussé decoration
above, an elaborate floral pattern and, below, a large scarb
beetle. L 45; D (disc) 24·5.

> *Bibliography: Necropolis* III, 20, 77f., no.135, pls.121, 273.
> Cyprus Museum, Nicosia.

233 Bronze side pendant ornament

Archaic period (about 700 BC)

Salamis, 'Royal' Tomb 79; Department of Antiquities
excavations.

Three components, all hinged and decorated in repoussé.
The goddess Ishtar stands on lions and holds a lion in each
hand with other animals around her and a winged sun disc
above. On the longer rectangular plate five panels showing
lions attacking bulls. On the top element and ridges. L (rect.
plate) 20, (smaller plate) 5, (disc) 29·5; W (rect. plate) 10,
(smaller plate) 6·5; H (total) 5·8.

> *Bibliography: Necropolis* III, 21f., 83f., nos. 155, 162,
> pls. 89, 272.
> Cyprus Museum, Nicosia.

232

233

234 Bronze breast plate
Archaic period (about 700 BC)
Salamis, 'Royal' Tomb 79; Department of Antiquities excavations.
Crescent shaped to fit the horse's neck, with perforations around the edge. Decorated in repoussé with two registers of figures, genii and fantastic animals. In the centre a four-winged genius holds a goat; above him is an elaborate tree design, itself below a winged sun disc. Round the edge a frieze of winged palmettes. Partly damaged; decoration very worn. H 47; D (at top) 50.
Bibliography: Necropolis III, 23, 84ff., no. 164, pls. 94, 95, 278.
Cyprus Museum, Nicosia.

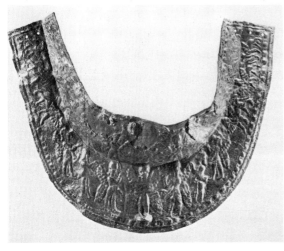

234

235a, b Two bronze bells
Archaic period (about 700 BC)
Salamis, 'Royal' Tomb 79; Department of Antiquities excavations.
Each has an iron clapper and loop for suspension. H a 8·5; b 9·2.
They originally hung from peytrels (neckbands) around the horse's neck.
Bibliography: Necropolis III, 35, 76, nos. 239–240, pls. 77, 265.
Cyprus Museum, Nicosia.

236 Two bronze yoke standards
Archaic period (675–625 BC)
Salamis, 'Royal' Tomb 79; Department of Antiquities excavations.

235b

236

Tubular shaft with loops at the bottom crowned by a disc with five long petals in the shape of a flower joined together by horizontal strips. H 50.

Bibliography: Necropolis III, 35, 76, nos. 239–240, pls. 77, 265.

Cyprus Museum, Nicosia.

237 Bronze hub-cap with iron lynch pin

Archaic period (about 700 BC)

Salamis, 'Royal' Tomb 79; Department of Antiquities excavations.

Hub-cap in the form of the head of a sphinx, the hair arranged in an Egyptian *klaft* (wig) and the eyes originally inlaid. Iron lynch pin pierced through the back of the wig. Cylindrical bronze attachment on top of the pin to hold the

237

238

bronze warrior figure (no. 238). L (pin) 16; H (of whole including no. 238) 56.

Bibliography: Necropolis III, 29, 80, no. 220/4, 4A, figs. 10, 11, pls. 103, 104.

Cyprus Museum, Nicosia.

238 Bronze soldier figurine, originally attached to the lynch pin, no. 237.

Archaic period (about 700 BC)

Salamis, 'Royal' Tomb 79: Department of Antiquities excavations.

Soldier standing bare-foot on a plinth with the left leg advanced. He wears a crested helmet and short-sleeved scale-corselet over a short tunic with engraved decoration. Both arms are bent forward. In his left hand he holds a sword which is stuck under his arm and hangs from a strap over his shoulder. Corroded, particularly the right hand. H (of figure) 29·5, (of whole) 26·5.

Bibliography: Necropolis III, 24, 80f., no. 188, fig. 10, pls. G, 103–105, 254, 257.
Cyprus Museum, Nicosia.

239 Bronze disc
Archaic period (about 700 BC)
Salamis, 'Royal' Tomb 79; Department of Antiquities excavations.
Originally attached at the end of one of the two chariot poles. Ovoid with a large perforation to hold the pole. Decorated in repoussé with a winged griffin striding to the left over a fallen man. H 31·5; D (max.) 24·5.
Bibliography: Necropolis III, 29, 81, no. 220/1, figs. 10, 11, pls. 107–8.
Cyprus Museum, Nicosia.

240b

239

240a-c Three bronze lion heads
Archaic period (about 700 BC)
Salamis, 'Royal' Tomb 79; Department of Antiquities excavations.
Hollow cast. Originally attached along the edge of the cart (hearse) floor by means of the rectangular sockets at the back. H **a, b** (of head) 10, (of socket) 8·8; H **c** (of head) 11·7, (of socket) 7·2.
Bibliography: Necropolis III, 32f., 60, 76, nos. 221/1, 6, 10, figs. 5–9, pls. 114–116, 261.
Cyprus Museum, Nicosia.

241 Bronze spearhead
Archaic period (about 700 BC)
Salamis, 'Royal' Tomb 79; Department of Antiquities excavations.
Large leaf-shaped blade with four grooves around the edge. Hollow tubular socket narrowing towards the blade with ridges at the junction and also at the upper end. Six disc-headed rivets at the end for attachment to wooden shaft. L 49; Max. W (of blade) 8; Max. D (of socket) 3·5.
Bibliography: Necropolis III, 19f., 118, no. 130, pls. 57, 266.
Cyprus Museum, Nicosia.

242 Silver bowl
Archaic period (700–600 BC)
Salamis, 'Royal' Tomb 2; Department of Antiquities excavations.
Shallow bowl; engraved decoration on the inside executed twice, the second scene superimposed on the first. Decoration A shows a pair of Egyptianising figures to the right in the central medallion surrounded by four concentric zones: in the outer, stylized papyrus flowers; in the second, nonsensical hieroglyphs; in the third, papyrus flowers; and in the inner, stemmed papyri. The second scene (decoration B) shows a winged sphinx to the right in the central medallion surrounded by three concentric zones: in the outer, opposed sphinxes; in the second, an egg pattern; and in the inner, elaborate lozenge motifs. D 14·5; H 3·8.

241

Bibliography: Necropolis I, 14, 19f., no. 71, pls. 10–12, 112–113, 116.
Cyprus Museum, Nicosia.

243 Iron horse-bit

Archaic period (650–600 BC)
Salamis, 'Royal' Tomb 2; Department of Antiquities excavations.
Consists of two horizontal twisted bars joined together by loops and inserted through a pair of flat cheek pieces, decorated with H-shaped projections. The projections are perforated to hold horse trappings. The tips of one cheekpiece and one of the perforations on the second cheekpiece are missing. L (of bar) 30, (of cheekpieces) 19·5.
Bibliography: Necropolis I, 14, 21, no. 54, pls. 15, 114.
Cyprus Museum, Nicosia.

244a, b Two bronze blinkers

Archaic period (650–600 BC)
Salamis, 'Royal' Tomb 3; Department of Antiquities excavations.
Sole-shaped with three pairs of perforations around the edge. Decorated in repoussé with a stemmed lotus bud. An ivory 'eye' is set in a hollow in the bud attached by a rivet in its centre, which is covered by dark paste to indicate the eyeball.
a L 21·3; W (max.) 8·8.
Bibliography: Necropolis I, 35, 48, no. 20, pls. 47, 127.
b L 22·2; W (max.) 8·5.
Bibliography: Ibid., 36, 48, no. 26, pls. 47, 127.
Cyprus Museum, Nicosia.

245 Silver-studded iron sword

Archaic period (about 600 BC)
Salamis, 'Royal' Tomb 3; Department of Antiquities excavations.
Leaf-shaped blade with low midrib and shallow grooves on either side. Fish-tail tang. Handle with round pommel attached to the tang by five bronze rivets with silver heads. This bronze border covered by silver around edge of tang. Traces of scabbard visible on surface of sword. L 92 (tang and pommel) 23; W (max. of tang) 10.
Bibliography: Necropolis I, 38, 43, no. 95, pls. 45, 129.
Cyprus Museum, Nicosia.

246 Terracotta vessel, perhaps an incense burner

Archaic period (700–600 BC)
Salamis, Cellarka cemetery, Tomb 23; Department of Antiquities excavations.
Deep bowl on a hollow cylindrical stem decorated with four draped female figures in relief standing with their arms by their sides. The women have black hair, red faces and arms and yellow drapery. Bowl decorated on the outside with a frieze of lotus flowers and buds in yellow outlined in black. Base partly restored. H 23; D (of bowl mouth) 12·5.
Bibliography: Necropolis II, 48, 52, no. 5, pls. B.1, 104, 221.
Cyprus Museum, Nicosia.

247 East Greek cup (skyphos)

Archaic period (700–650 BC)
Salamis, Cellarka cemetery, Tomb 24; Department of Antiquities excavations.

Handle zone on either side divided into three panels by groups of vertical bands. Bird to the right in the centre flanked by hatched lozenges. Radiating star on bottom. Black with reserved band below rim on inside. H 4·5; D 11.

Bird bowls were made in all the East Greek cities but probably originated in Rhodes. This is one of several found in Cyprus.

Bibliography: Necropolis II, 57f., no. 2, pls. 111, 223.
Cyprus Museum, Nicosia.

248 Terracotta bird
Archaic period (600–500 BC)
Salamis, Cellarka cemetery, Tomb 9; Department of Antiquities excavations.
Hand-made. Flying with outstretched wings on a conical base. Decorated with purple and black paint. L 9; H 6.

Bibliography: Necropolis II, 56, no. 9, pls. A.2, 109.
Cyprus Museum, Nicosia.

249 Terracotta horse and rider
Archaic period (600–500 BC)
Salamis, Cellarka Cemetery, Tomb 21; Department of Antiquities excavations.
Hand-made. The rider is bearded and wears a conical helmet. Both rider and horse are decorated with bands in dark red and purple matt paint. H 12.

Bibliography: Necropolis II, 45, no. 16, pls. B.4, 92.
Cyprus Museum, Nicosia.

250 Terracotta dog
Archaic period (600–500 BC)
Salamis, Cellarka cemetery, Tomb 27A; Department of Antiquities excavations.
Hand-made. Decorated with bands in black and purple matt paint. L 9·5; H 7.

Bibliography: Necropolis II, 56, no. 8, pls. A.2, 109.
Cyprus Museum, Nicosia.

251 Terracotta warrior
Archaic period (600–500 BC)
Salamis, Cellarka cemetery, Tomb 85A; Department of Antiquities excavations.
Hand-made. He wears a pointed cap and stands on a conical base with his arms folded forward. Black and purple for features and stripes on arms and base. H 12·5.

Bibliography: Necropolis II, 131, no. 11, pl. 167.
Cyprus Museum, Nicosia.

252 Terracotta boat
Archaic period (600–500 BC)
Salamis, Cellarka cemetery, Tomb 104; Department of Antiquities excavations.
Hand-made. A bearded male figure, wearing a pointed cap with his arms outstretched to hold the sides, sits in the boat. Purple spots on left arm. L 10; H 4·2.

Bibliography: Necropolis II, 149f., no. 5, pl. 176.
Cyprus Museum, Nicosia.

253 Terracotta shield
Archaic/Classical period (about 475 BC)
Salamis, Cellarka cemetery, Tomb 13; Department of Antiquities excavations.
Conical with central boss in the shape of a lion's head. Blue, black and yellow bands around boss. Hand grip missing. D 21·5.

Bibliography: Necropolis II, 29f., no. 41, pls. B.5, 74, 211.
Cyprus Museum, Nicosia.

Kition

This town, known as Kittim in the Bible, had a Late Bronze Age predecessor but it had finally been abandoned in the early Geometric period about 1000 BC. The Phoenicians arrived at Kition in the middle of the ninth century BC when they were beginning their westward expansion. They were responsible for the re-birth of the town which had been abandoned for a century and a half. Finds of the later Geometric period are included here with the archaic objects since they all belong to this new phase in the city's history which has been revealed in area II by the Department of Antiquities of Cyprus since 1962. The Phoenicians built a temple dedicated to the goddess Astarte on the foundations of the largest of the Late Bronze Age temples and they restored two others, thus maintaining the sacred area at the northernmost part of the town. On the acropolis of Kition, situated on the Bamboula hill south-east of area II overlooking the ancient harbour, were two sanctuaries dedicated to Heracles-Melqart, the patron god of Kition, and to Aphrodite-Astarte.

Inscriptions (nos. 257, 259) and offerings, including the Egyptianising bronze statues (nos. 260, 261) and the faience vase and amulet (nos. 263, 264), which the Phoenicians may have brought with them, bear witness to the strong Phoenician impact on Kition. This influence extended in the Classical period to other places when Kition ruled over Tamassos and Idalion. At its height it reached as far west as Amathus and to Lapithos on the north coast, and there was a time in the fifth century BC when even Salamis had a Phoenician king. In 312 BC, however, the last king of Kition, Poumiathon, was killed by Ptolemy of Egypt and thus the Phoenician dynasty at Kition was brought to an end. [V.K.]

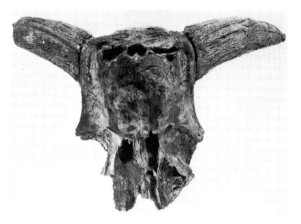

254

Bibliography: Karageorghis (1976), 102ff., pls. 80–81 Cyprus Museum, Nicosia. Skull A.

255, 256 Ten miniature vases
Geometric period (about 800 BC)
Kition, from a *bothros* (pit) in the south-east corner of the Phoenician temple of Astarte; Department of Antiquities excavations.

This deposit included numerous miniature vases of which these ten are a selection. Many were found intact and other finds in the same *bothros* included animal bones, an iron skewer and a knife. Since they are covered directly by the foundations of the rebuilt temple these finds may form a foundation deposit.

Bibliography: Karageorghis (1976), 108, pls. xvii, xviii.

255 Five jugs, Black-on-Red ware
Decorated with bands and concentric circles. H 5·5–8·8.
Cyprus Museum, Nicosia. Kition, area II/2111, 2116, 2117, 2159, 2173.

254 Skull of an oxen
Geometric period (850–800 BC)
Kition, from the courtyard of the Phoenician temple of Astarte; Department of Antiquities excavations.
H 14·5.

Skulls were worn in religious ceremonies at least from the Late Bronze Age and bucrania decorate Early Bronze Age sanctuary models (as nos. 54, 55). The practice is also illustrated by the terracotta group from Kourion (no. 267).

255

255

256

256 Four bowls and one jug, Grey Polished ware
H 4·1–7·4; D 6–15·6 (bowls); H 14·1 (jug).

Cyprus Museum, Nicosia. Kition, area II/2119, 2120, 2128, 2136, 2188.

257 Bowl with Phoenician inscription, Red Slip ware
Geometric period (about 800 BC)
Kition, from the court of the Phoenician temple of Astarte; Department of Antiquities excavations.

257

Dedication in six lines to the goddess Astarte by a citizen of Tamassos. Considerably restored. H 5·8; D (reconstructed) 25.

The inscription reads, line (1) In Memorial. ML had his hair (herein) shaved and prayed to Lady Astarte and Astarte listened to his prayer (2) And were offered (as a sacrifice): on the part of ML, a sheep and a lamb, together (3) with this hair; on the part of the family of ML, a lamb. This vase (4) ML filled with his hair (herein) . . . seven in number, because of the prayer made in Tamassos (5) . . . The gift . . . which he liked . . . (6) Tamassos.

The bowl is of imported Phoenician Red Slip ware and the dedication is particularly important since it describes part of the ritual associated with the worship of Astarte at Kition.

Bibliography: Karageorghis (1976), 106f., pl. 83; *Kition* III, 149ff., no. D21, pl. 17.1–2, fig. 23.

Cyprus Museum, Nicosia. Kition, area II/1435.

258 Bowl with syllabic inscription, Red Slip ware
Archaic period (725–700 BC)
Kition, pit *(bothros)* to the east of the Phoenician temple of Astarte; Department of Antiquities excavations.
Inscription incised after firing. Fragment. H 13·6; D (original) 7·5.

The bowl itself is of the imported Red Slip fabric. The inscription seems to be complete reading, from right to left, *Ta-su-mi-ne-mo,* which appears to be Eteo-Cypriote rather than Greek. Only a very few syllabic inscriptions of the end of the eighth century are known.

Bibliography: Karageorghis, *BCH* XCV (1971), 379, fig. 86A.

Cyprus Museum, Nicosia. Kition, area II/2359.

259 Bowl with Phoenician inscription, Bichrome Red ware
Archaic period (600–500 BC)
Kition; Department of Antiquities excavations.

259

260   262   263   264

Inscription incised after firing; dedication to Melqart. H 5; D (reconstructed) 10.

The Phoenician god Melqart at Tyre was synonymous with Baal (meaning 'Lord'). This bowl, unlike nos. 257 and 258, is of local manufacture and the inscription simply names the god.

Bibliography: *Kition* III, 167f., no. D34, pl. 23.5.

Cyprus Museum, Nicosia. Kition, area II/3215.

260 Bronze statuette

Archaic period (700–600 BC)

Kition, outside the Phoenician temple of Astarte; Department of Antiquities excavations.

Cast solid. He wears an Egyptian crown and kilt and stands with left leg advanced and both arms by his sides. H 5.

Bibliography: Karageorghis, *BCH* XCIV (1970), 255, fig. 109; *idem*, (1976) 111, pl. xix.

Cyprus Museum, Nicosia. Kition, area II/1934.

261 Bronze statuette

Archaic period (700–600 BC)

Kition, outside the Phoenician temple of Astarte; Department of Antiquities excavations.

Cast solid. As no. 260 except that the right arm is raised in a gesture of benediction.

Bibliography: Karageorghis, *BCH* XCIV (1970), 255; *idem* (1976) 111, pl. 84.

Cyprus Museum, Nicosia. Kition, area II/1920.

262 Terracotta female bust

Archaic period (600–450 BC)

Kition, pit (*bothros*) outside the Phoenician temple of Astarte; Department of Antiquities excavations.

Her hair is arranged in curls over her forehead with two locks falling forward onto her shoulders; she wears a low crown (or *polos*) and a necklace. H 4.9.

Bibliography: Karageorghis, *BCH* XCV (1971), 379, fig. 88.

Cyprus Museum, Nicosia. Kition, area II/2370.

263 Faience vase, greenish blue painted in green or blue and yellow.

Archaic period (800–600 BC)

Kition, from the court of the Phoenician temple of Astarte; Department of Antiquities excavations.

In the form of a kneeling woman. She wears a tall hat (*kalathos*) and an elaborate garment. On her back is a child in a kind of sack and on her knees she holds a goat. She rests on a rectangular plinth in front of which is a lion's head. Openings for pouring liquid in the top of the *kalathos* and through the mouth of the lion. W (max.) 2.6; H (total) 7.04; TH (max. of socket) 3.77.

This flask may have been used to carry the 'water of the Nile'. Several examples have been found both in Egypt itself and in the Greek world, notably in the islands of Rhodes and Samos and at Perachora near Corinth. Others come from Etruscan tombs and it seems likely that they were transported by Phoenician traders although some, including this example, may have been manufactured in a Rhodian rather than Egyptian workshop.

Bibliography: Karageorghis, *BCH* XCIV (1970), 255, fig. 103; *Kition* II, 184ff., no. 1747, pl. 20.1–4, fig. 15.

Cyprus Museum, Nicosia.

264 Faience 'Bes' amulet

Archaic period (600–475 BC)

Kition, outside the Phoenician temple of Astarte; Department of Antiquities excavations.

Squatting, with his hands resting on his thighs; he wears a tall feathered crown and a lion-skin. w 2·1; h 6·6; Th 1·05.

Like the flask this faience amulet, one of several of the type from Kition, was probably brought there by the Phoenicians.

Bibliography: Karageorghis, *BCH* XCVI (1972), 1064, fig. 80; *Kition* II, 161, no. 2952, pl. 9.

Cyprus Museum, Nicosia.

Terracottas

In Iron Age Cyprus terracotta figures were made in great numbers mainly for dedication in sanctuaries. The typical Cypriote sanctuary consisted of a temenos *or open court, enclosed by a wall, with small cult buildings, maybe including a chapel, as well as perhaps an altar. The main sanctuaries had their own terracotta workshops, and it seems that the Cypriots believed that their dedications would act as substitutes for themselves as*

continuous worshippers. Some represent offering-bearers, others musicians evidently taking part in a ceremony. The cult of the sanctuary may also be recognised from the finds as at Ayia Irini and Meniko (nos. 214–297 below). The figures are made in various techniques but, when decorated, the same colour and styles as the contemporary vases are used for them all. The smaller pieces may be hand-modelled, the so-called 'snowman' figures (e.g. nos. 251, 267, 274), or have a trumpet-shaped body, either made by hand or on a wheel, with a hand-modelled head like the earlier examples (e.g. nos. 269, 276–278). The use of the mould reached the island from Syria in the eighth century, and Cyprus may have played some part in introducing it to Greece soon after 700 BC. There are many moulded plaques and figurines of the Archaic period. Some of the latter are still fairly small with a moulded head on a wheel-made body (e.g. no. 283) but particularly remarkable are the large examples, sometimes over life-size, made up of separate pieces. They follow in style the contemporary sculpture (e.g. nos. 279–282).

[V.A.T.-B.]

265 Terracotta shrine model

Archaic period (700–600 BC)

Unknown provenance.

A small, roughly square building with a rectangular door and three small windows. Inside a seated figure is playing a lyre. Before him a stump for a table or perhaps a sacred tree. Small figures climb up the sides to look into the room. Wheel-made with the walls pushed in. Traces of brown and red paint. Fragmentary. W 10·4; H 11.

> *Bibliography:* Boardman, *RDAC* (1971), 37ff., pl. 17.
> Cyprus Museum, Nicosia. B220.

266 Terracotta harpist

Archaic period (about 600 BC)

Unknown provenance.

She is wearing elaborate jewellery and a low cap. Her mouth is half-open perhaps showing that she is singing. Hand-made with solid cylindrical body and modelled head. H 19.

> *Bibliography:* Karageorghis (1962), 20, pl. 30.
> Cyprus Museum, Nicosia. B191.

267 Group of terracotta figures wearing bulls' masks

Archaic period (650–600 BC)

Temple of Apollo at Kourion; American excavations.

Two figures are preserved and there are remains for the attachment of three more. They are evidently moving clockwise with their arms raised to hold their bulls' masks. Hand-made with solid tubular bodies. Broken and some figures missing; two fragments. L 11·1; W 9; H 9·7.

> *Bibliography:* Young (1955), 40, no. 814, pl. 11; Karageorghis (1976), 105, pl. 82.
> Cyprus Museum, Nicosia. Kourion, T1775.

268 Terracotta female head

Archaic period (about 600 BC)

Unknown provenance.

Probably from a statuette of a woman holding a vase on her head. Richly decorated in black paint, the features also indicated and bands on her neck and hair. Hollow, moulded. Broken at top and bottom. H 16·6.

> *Bibliography:* J. Karageorghis (1977), 144, pl. 24e; Karageorghis, *Scripta Minora* (Lund 1977), 21f., pl. 8.3, 4.
> Cyprus Museum, Nicosia. 1938/IV–83.

268a Terracotta goddess with uplifted arms

Archaic period (600–500 BC)

From near Palapaphos.

Hand-made trumpet-shaped body, modelled breasts and nose. She wears a tall hat. H 7·5.

> *Bibliography:* BCH XCII (1968), 287, fig. 58.
> Paphos Museum. 1788.

265

266

267

268

269 Terracotta warrior

Archaic period (700–600 BC)

Unknown provenance.

He holds a shield on his left arm and his right arm is raised. Decorated in bichrome technique with matt black and purplish red bands on body, features indicated, and wheel pattern on the shield with red boss. Cylindrical wheel-made body and hand-made head. H 17·6.

Bibliography: Dikaios (1961), 206, no. 58, pl. 30·7.

Cyprus Museum, Nicosia. B40.

Illustrated in colour.

270 Terracotta chariot

Archaic period (700–600 BC)

Tjónia, near Ovgoros.

Two-horsed vehicle carrying the driver and a warrior, both bearded and wearing pointed helmets, the latter equipped with a spiked shield. Leading the two horses is a third figure walking between them. He is also bearded and wearing a helmet and short tunic. Hand-made. Partly broken. L 14·3; W 10; H 16·8.

Bibliography: Megaw, *Arch. Rep.* for 1955, 43, pl. 2d; Littauer-Crouwel, *AA* (1977), 7f., figs. 3–6.

Cyprus Museum, Nicosia. 1955/IX–26/1.

271 Terracotta chariot

Archaic period (700–600 BC)

Unknown provenance.

Model with large wheels and round body over the top of which looks a figure. Decorated in bichrome technique with semi-circles on the sides of the cab and a bird in the middle. Broken and mended. W 16·5; H 12·5.

These brightly decorated vehicles were probably toys.

Bibliography: Karageorghis, *BCH* XC (1966), 114f., fig. 12; Karageorghis and des Gagniers (1974), 67, no. XXVd. 18, pl. 354.

Cyprus Museum, Nicosia. B4.

271

272 Terracotta horse and rider
Archaic period (700–600 BC)
Unknown provenance. Formerly in the Hadjiprodromou collection.
Richly decorated in purple and black paint. H 17.
    Bibliography: Karageorghis, *BCH* CII (1978), 881, fig. 5.
Cyprus Museum, Nicosia. 1977/VIII–23/5.

273 Terracotta horse's head
Archaic period (700–600 BC)
Peyia, Kambos tis Maaas.
Harness and trappings indicated in relief and by incision. L 7; H 8·4.
    Bibliography: Karageorghis, *BCH* LXXXVIII (1964), 323, fig. 49.
    Paphos Museum. 1691/37.

273

Ayia Irini

This sanctuary, near the coast in north-west Cyprus, was excavated by the Swedish expedition in 1929. It is particularly remarkable for the large number of terracottas (about 2000) discovered around the altar in the temenos. The sanctuary itself was in use from the end of the Late Bronze Age until about 500 BC when it was destroyed by a flood, but it flourished particularly in the seventh and early sixth centuries when most of the statues in this exhibition, which represent only a very small proportion of the whole, were offered. The sanctuary was probably dedicated to the god of fertility whose rites included worship by priests in bulls' masks (see no. 267). The number of war chariots (like nos. 285–287) and armed figures (nos. 280–282) suggest that the fertility god became also a god of war. [V.A.T.-B.]

274 Terracotta male statuette
Archaic period (700–600 BC)
Ayia Irini; Swedish excavations.
Standing bearded male with arms by his side. He wears a conical helmet and a mantle draped back over his shoulders. Folds of the mantle indicated by incisions. Hand-made with solid body. Traces of black on beard. H 43·8.
    Bibliography: SCE II, 707, no. 1062, pl. 231·15.
Cyprus Museum, Nicosia.

275 Terracotta male statue
Archaic period (660–600 BC)
Ayia Irini; Swedish excavations.
Bearded figure wearing a helmet and long girdled tunic with modelled folds below the girdle. Tubular body, wheel-made in two halves. Features painted black. Partly broken and restored. H 187.
    Bibliography: SCE II, 753f., nos. 2106, 2103, pls. 190, 192·1.
Cyprus Museum, Nicosia.

276 Terracotta male statuette
Archaic period (660–600 BC)
Ayia Irini; Swedish excavations.
Dressed in a tunic and mantle draped over both shoulders and a conical helmet. He stands with his arms by his sides. Tubular wheel-made body, hand-modelled head. Traces of

274

275

277   282   283

black and red on features and drapery. Hands missing, partly broken. H 85.

 Bibliography: SCE II, 731, no. 1566, pl. 195·1–2.
 Cyprus Museum, Nicosia.

277 Terracotta male statuette
Archaic period (660–600 BC)
Ayia Irini; Swedish excavations.
Male figure wearing a pointed helmet with tassel and a fringed mantle draped over the left shoulder. Tubular wheel-made body and hand-made head. Partly broken; lower right arm and hand missing. H 55·6.

 Bibliography: SCE II, 727, no. 1505, pl. 238·5.
 Cyprus Museum, Nicosia.

278 Terracotta male statuette
Archaic period (660–600 BC)
Ayia Irini; Swedish excavations.

Bearded figure in a tall helmet wearing a tunic with a girdle below which appear ridged folds. Stands with arms by his sides. Tubular wheel-made body, hand-modelled head. Black paint on hair, beard and drapery. H 55·8.

 Bibliography: SCE II, 742, no. 1805, pl. 237·3.
 Cyprus Museum, Nicosia.

279 Terracotta male statue
Archaic period (660–600 BC)
Ayia Irini; Swedish excavations.
Bearded figure wearing a helmet, tunic and mantle draped over both shoulders. Folds of tunic shown by incision over the feet. Body hand-made in two parts, arms attached separately. Traces of black and red on drapery and features. Partly broken; lower right arm missing. H 177·4.

 Bibliography: SCE II, 737, no. 1727, pl. 211.
 Cyprus Museum, Nicosia.

280 Terracotta warrior

Archaic period (660–600 BC)

Ayia Irini; Swedish excavations.

He wears a helmet and short tunic with a sword tucked under his left arm. Hand-made in two halves with legs and arms attached separately. Traces of black on features. H 177·7.

Bibliography: SCE II, 753, no. 2102, pl. 202.

Cyprus Museum, Nicosia.

281 Terracotta warrior

Archaic period (660–600 BC)

Ayia Irini; Swedish excavations.

Male figure in tall spiked helmet wearing a short girdled tunic and standing with left leg advanced. Hand-made head and feet attached separately. H 91.

Bibliography: SCE II, 739f., no. 1767, pls. 205·1, 206·1, 5.

Cyprus Museum, Nicosia.

282 Terracotta warrior

Archaic period (660–600 BC)

Ayia Irini; Swedish excavations.

Equipped with shield and spear and wearing a tall helmet and short tunic. He stands with left leg slightly advanced. Hand-made with legs and arms attached separately. H 53·6.

Bibliography: SCE II, 721f., nos. 1385, 1530, pl. 194. 2.

Cyprus Museum, Nicosia.

283 Terracotta male statuette

Archaic period (600–550 BC)

Ayia Irini; Swedish excavations.

He wears a helmet and stands with his left arm by his side and his right held across the body in the fold of his mantle. Wheel-made body in two halves, head moulded, hand-made feet, arms and hands. Traces of black and red paint indicating the folds and borders of the drapery. Neck and left shoulder broken. H 84·5.

Bibliography: SCE II, 707, nos. 1052, 2442, pl. 219. 2, 4.

Cyprus Museum, Nicosia.

284 Terracotta female statuette

Archaic period (700–600 BC)

Ayia Irini; Swedish excavations.

Woman seated in a chair supported by a pair of winged sphinxes with their feathers indicated by incised striped rectangles and squares. Hand-made. Partly broken, head of sphinx and lower left arm of woman missing. L (of sphinxes) 20; W (max) 29; H (of woman) 28.6.

Thrones supported by sphinxes were popular in Phoenicia from the Late Bronze Age whence they were adopted by the Cypriots. These particular sphinxes with their double curved wings growing from the centre of the body and cap-like

284

head-dress, if not a local variation, have their closest parallels in Syria.

Bibliography: SCE II, 731, nos. 1563, 2026, pl. 233·10–11.

Cyprus Museum, Nicosia.

285 Terracotta chariot

Archaic period (700–600 BC)

Ayia Irini; Swedish excavations.

Vehicle drawn by four horses with elaborate trappings. It carries three people: the driver with both hands holding the reins, a warrior, perhaps with a bow (now missing), and, behind him, a second warrior with a shield. Hand-made. Considerably broken and mended. H 14·7; L 23·9; W 15·3.

Bibliography: SCE II, 740, no. 1780, pl. 234·3.

Cyprus Museum, Nicosia.

286 Terracotta chariot

Archaic period (700–600 BC)

Ayia Irini; Swedish excavations.

Four-horsed chariot similar to no. 285, carrying the driver and a warrior equipped with a shield. A second warrior with a shield stands at the back trying to mount the vehicle. Hand-made. Parts missing and broken. L 27·5; W 23·3; H 23·7.

Bibliography: SCE II, 740f., nos. 1781, 798, pl. 235·3.

Cyprus Museum, Nicosia.

286

287 Terracotta chariot

Archaic period (700–600 BC)

Ayia Irini; Swedish excavations.

Four-horsed chariot carrying the driver and a warrior equipped with a spiked shield and a spear which he holds ready to throw. On the side of the chariot a bow and a quiver full of arrows. Hand-made. Traces of blue, red and yellow paint. Parts missing and broken. L 20·5; W 21·7; H 22.6.

Bibliography: SCE II, 748, no. 2000, pl. 234·5.

Cyprus Museum, Nicosia.

288–290 Three terracotta 'centaurs'

Ayia Irini; Swedish excavations.

288 Archaic period (about 750 BC)

Body of a bull with a human torso. Beardless head wearing a pointed helmet; torso dressed in a short skirt. Female breasts below the armpits. Left arm raised and holding a snake by the head. Partly wheel-made. Broken; right arm and other parts missing. H 32·3; L 13·5.

Bibliography: SCE II, 749, nos. 2031, 2361, pl. 227·1; Karageorghis, Χαριστηριον εις Ἀταστασιον κ. Ὀρλανδον part B (1966), 164ff., pl. 24a.

Cyprus Museum, Nicosia.

289 Archaic period (about 600 BC)

As no. 290, with the body of a bull and human torso. Bearded horned head with incised lines for hair on forehead and long spiral curls falling down on each shoulder. Arms bent and outstretched. Wheel-made body and legs, hand-modelled arms and head. Traces of black paint. Partly broken. L 16·5; H 28·1.

Bibliography: SCE II, 710f., no. 1122, pl. 228·5; Karageorghis, *op.cit.* pl. 23b.

Cyprus Museum, Nicosia.

290 Archaic period (about 600 BC)

As no. 289, with the body of a bull and human torso. Bearded head, the torso dressed in a tunic. Arms outstretched before him. Snakes coil up from the animal body on to the head. Wheel-made body and legs, hand-made arms and head. Traces of black and red on features and hind-legs. H 63·9; L 51.

Bibliography: SCE II, 753, no. 2101, pl. 2281·1; Karageorghis, *op.cit.* pl. 23a.

Cyprus Museum, Nicosia.

These are appropriate offerings in the Ayia Irini sanctuary which was dedicated to a fertility god one of whose main attributes was the bull. In technique they recall the Enkomi

290

centaur (no. 106 above) and there is some evidence that votive animals with wheel-made bodies continued to be made in Cyprus during the Geometric period (e.g. no. 185) as they did in Crete. However, the reappearance of a half-human, half-animal figure in Cyprus after a gap of three centuries is probably due to influence from the Greek world where there are a limited number of early examples including a fine true centaur with equine body (Desborough, *et. al.*, *BSA* LXV (1970), 21ff., pls. 7–11).

Meniko

The finds from this sanctuary include many fine terracottas dating from the sixth century BC. Most important is the ram-headed god who is associated with incense burners (nos. 291–294) and has therefore been identified as Baal-Hamman (god of the perfume altar) to whom the sanctuary was dedicated. [V.A.T.–B.]

291 Terracotta ram-headed god
Archaic period (600–500 BC)
Meniko sanctuary; Department of Antiquities excavations.
Seated on a throne and dressed in a full-length tunic and sandals. W (throne) 7·6; H (total) 18·5, (throne) 10·5.

This figure has been identified as Baal-Hamman the god to whom the Meniko sanctuary was dedicated. He is a combination of the Phoenician god Baal to whom dedications were made at Kition (no. 259) and the Libyan ram god Ammon,

291

292   294

ported a double bowl with a lid as shown here. Both the bowls are conical with straight sides and a plain rim. The common flat base has a depression in the centre. Decoration in matt black shows a lattice pattern on the lower bowl and vertical bands on the upper bowl. The conical lid is perforated and has a basket handle. It is decorated with a lattice pattern in black and purple. H 57.
  Bibliography: Karageorghis (1977), 28f., 39ff., nos. 21 + 26, 33, fig. 7, pls. A, 12.
  Cyprus Museum, Nicosia.

294 Terracotta incense burner (thymiaterion)
Archaic period (600–500 BC)
Similar to no. 293. The stand is virtually identical. The double bowl comprises a shallow bowl with straight sides and plain rim below a bowl with carinated sides and flat sloping rim. The common base has a depression in the centre. It is decorated in black with a lattice pattern on the upper bowl and ahtick band below the rim on the lower bowl. The lid is as the last and is decorated in black and purple with four large latticed triangles. H 59.
  Bibliography: Karageorghis (1977), 28, 39ff., nos. 22 + 23 + 34, fig. 7, pls. A, 12.
  Cyprus Museum, Nicosia.

295 Terracotta group, a bull accompanied by two men
Archaic period (600–500 BC)
Meniko; Department of Antiquities excavations.
H (of bull) 28·5.
  This bull is probably being led to sacrifice, as that on the chariot, no. 103.
  Bibliography: Karageorghis (1977), 27, 37, no. 16, pl. 10.
  Cyprus Museum, Nicosia.
  Illustrated in colour.

296 Terracotta male statuette
Archaic period (600–550 BC)
Meniko; Department of Antiquities excavations.
He wears a pointed helmet, short-sleeved vest and shorts with rosette belt. Moulded with a flat back. Legs below knees missing. H 35.
  Bibliography: Karageorghis (1977), 25, 36, no. 2, pl. 7.
  Cyprus Museum, Nicosia.

297 Terracotta ritual vessel ('kernos')
Archaic period (600–500 BC)
Meniko; Department of Antiquities excavations.
Consists of three bowls with lids joined together with a wishbone handle at either end. L 20·5; H 9·5.
  Bibliography: Karageorghis (1977), 30, 42, no. 45, pl. 13, fig. 10.
  Cyprus Museum, Nicosia.

but he was also worshipped as Baal Hamman (literally 'god of the perfume altar') in Phoenicia itself as well as in the western Phoenician (later Punic) centre of Carthage.
  Bibliography: Karageorghis (1977), 24f., 35f., no. 1, pls. 6, 29.
  Cyprus Museum, Nicosia.

292 Limestone incense burner (thymiaterion)
Archaic period (600–500 BC)
Meniko; Department of Antiquities excavations.
A bowl with conical lid and biconical knob on the top rests on a stand with a conical foot. Decorated with horizontal parallel bands and rings in black, purple and green. H 55·1; D (bowl) 10.
  Bibliography: Karageorghis (1977), 34, 39f., nos. 101, 102, pl. 12, fig. 7.
  Cyprus Museum, Nicosia.

293 Terracotta incense burner (thymiaterion)
Archaic period (600–500 BC)
Meniko; Department of Antiquities excavations.
A stand supports a double bowl with a conical lid. The stand has a hollow cylindrical stem with a row of petals around the top, below a globe on which rests the support for the upper part. It is decorated in black and purple with vertical bands and, on the lower part, a lattice pattern. It probably sup-

Vases

The vases in particular illustrate the regional divisions in Archaic Cyprus. The principal wares, White Painted, Bichrome, Black-on-Red, Red Slip and Black or Grey Polished, are found all over the island, but it is in the decoration that the differences can be observed. The 'western style', concentrated in the north and west, employs elaborate circle designs drawn with compasses (e.g. no. 308), a development of the late geometric ornaments illustrated by the miniature vases from Kition (no. 255). The 'eastern style' of the south and east is characterised by elaborate geometric and floral motifs including the guilloche, lotus flowers and open palmettes and, above all, by fine pictorial compositions, perhaps seen at their best on the 'free-field' style jugs (e.g. nos. 299–301). The eastern school is the more attractive, its iconography is derived from both Syrian and Phoenician sources including textiles and objects of ivory or precious metal, which, whether imported or made locally, are ultimately of Phoenician origin.

Not all foreign influence is from the Near East. Imported Greek pottery is found, in particular at Marion, but this is mostly from the East Greek world (e.g. nos. 247, 312, 313). Occasionally the style is imitated by the Cypriots themselves (e.g. no. 310).　　　[V.A.T.–B.]

299

298 Barrel jug, Bichrome ware
Archaic period (750–650 BC)
Gypsos; purchased.
Body divided into zones by vertical concentric circles. In the centre opposite the handle a large bird to the right. On either side a bull each walking up the vase towards a large flower. H 30·5.

Bibliography: Dikaios, *RDAC* (1937–9), 135, no. 4, pl. 39.4–5, figs. 1–2; Karageorghis and des Gagniers (1974), 67, no. XXV.b.27, pl. 3.5.

Cyprus Museum, Nicosia. 1938/X–4/1.

299 Jug, Bichrome ware
Archaic period (750–650 BC)
Arnadhi.
Decorated in the 'free-field' style in reddish purple and black with a bull moving to the left sniffing a lotus flower. Above, a rosette between vertical bands flanked by semi-circles. H 23·5.

300

Bibliography: Karageorghis and des Gagniers (1974), 48, XVI.b.14, pl. 166.
Cyprus Museum, Nicosia. 1951/IV–2/92f.

300 Jug, Bichrome ware
Archaic period (750–650 BC)
Unknown provenance.
Decorated in the 'free-field' style with an archer moving to the right shooting at a stag which stands before a plant. Behind him is a bull before a flower. H 28.
Bibliography: Karageorghis and des Gagniers (1974), Texte 18f., no. III.2, pls. 32–33.
Cyprus Museum, Nicosia B1949.

301 Jug, Bichrome ware
Archaic period (750–650 BC)
Unknown provenance; purchased.
Decorated in the 'free-field' style with a bird to the right before a stylised tree. H 22.
Bibliography: Dikaios, *RDAC* (1937–9), 143, no. 11, pl. 40.5; Karageorghis and des Gagniers (1974), Texte 68, no. XXV.f.8, pl. 392.
Cyprus Museum, Nicosia. 1938/IV–8/1.

302 Stemmed cup, Bichrome ware
Archaic period (750–650 BC)
Unknown provenance.
Decorated on the outside with panels of geometric motifs around the rim on both sides. On the body on one side a

302

frieze of fantastic birds to the right, and geometric motifs on the other. On the inside, chevron decoration around the rim and, below, a frieze of birds and goats; encircling bands around centre. H 16·5; D 24.

Bibliography: Dikaios, *RDAC* (1937–9), 137, no. 6, pl. 39.6; Karageorghis and des Gagniers (1974), Texte 50, no. XVII.25, pls. 192–3.
Cyprus Museum, Nicosia. 1939/XII–1/1.

303 Deep footed bowl (krater), Bichrome ware
Archaic period (750–650 BC)
Unknown provenance.
Deep bowl standing on three looped feet with double handles forming bulls' heads. Decorated in black and purplish red in panels on body. On one side, in the centre, a bird to the right bordered by groups of vertical lines. On the other side, panels filled with geometric and floral motifs. H 16·5; D (mouth) 13.
Bibliography: Karageorghis and des Gagniers (1974), Texte 67, no. XXVd.10, pl. 345.
Cyprus Museum, Nicosia. B1981.

304 Vase (krater), Bichrome ware
Archaic period (750–650 BC)
Unknown provenance.
On either side a panel in the handle zone decorated with three rows of utensils, jugs at the top and cups below with combs or trays between. H 20·8; D (mouth) 17.
Bibliography: Karageorghis and des Gagniers (1974), Texte 86, no. XXIX.4, pl. 498.
Cyprus Museum, Nicosia. B1992.

305 Vase (amphora), Bichrome ware
Archaic period (750–650 BC)
Unknown provenance.
Neck decorated with checks. On the shoulder on either side a pair of helmeted sphinxes confronting each other over a sacred tree. Bordered below by a frieze of meanders. Encircling bands around lower part of body. H 47·5; D (mouth) 25·5.
Bibliography: Karageorghis and des Gagniers (1974), Texte 39, no. XIIa.1, pl. 124.
Cyprus Museum, Nicosia. B2009.

306 Vase (amphora), Bichrome ware
Archaic period (about 600 BC)
Unknown provenance.
On the neck, panels filled with geometric motifs bordered above by a cable pattern and egg–and–dart motif. In the handle zone on each side a pair of opposing helmeted sphinxes confronting an elaborate floral motif. Geometric border to the left. Frieze of rosettes below. H 61; D (mouth) 29·5.
Bibliography: Karageorghis and des Gagniers (1974), Texte 39, no. XIIa.3, pl. 127f.
Cyprus Museum, Nicosia. B333.

307 Vase (hydria). Bichrome ware
Archaic period (750–650 BC)
Kourion region.
Neck in the form of a human face with features either painted or shown in relief. Group of encircling bands on body. Band around bottom of neck. H 17.
Bibliography: Karageorghis, *BCH* C (1976), 841, fig. 4.
Cyprus Museum, Nicosia. 1975/IX–29/3.

308 Vase in the form of a tortoise (askos), Bichrome ware
Archaic period (750–650 BC)
Unknown provenance; formerly Hadjiprodromou collection.
Biconical body with tubular opening on the top and basket handle. Tortoise head spout at one end. Five projections around lower part of body. Bichrome geometric decoration of four multiple triangles radiating towards the centre with semi-circles, bands and dots around neck. L 14·6; H 9·5.
Bibliography: Karageorghis, *BCH* XCIII (1969), 504, fig. 141a-b.
Cyprus Museum, Nicosia. 1977/VIII–23/6.

309 Hanging lamp, Bichrome ware
Archaic period (750–650 BC)
Unknown provenance; formerly Hadjiprodromou collection.
Terminates at the top in a bull's head. On the body, a warrior in three-quarter view to the left holding up an axe in his right hand. W 12·5; H 27·7.
Bibliography: Karageorghis, *Studi Fenici* III (1975), 165ff., pl. 36.
Cyprus Museum, Nicosia. 1977/VIII–23/14.

312

310 Jar, Bichrome ware
Archaic period (575–550 BC)
Goudhi.
Animals drawn in outline and silhouette with abstract filling ornaments. On one side, a bull confronting a lion behind which stands a duck. On the other side, a boar between two lions. H 31; D 39·4.
Both the animal style and filling ornaments are copied from Rhodian pottery of the early sixth century, but the shape is in the Cypriote repertoire.
Bibliography: Karageorghis, *BCH* CI (1977), 718, fig. 19.
Paphos Museum. 2235/1.

311 Tripod bowl
Archaic period (750–650 BC)
Unknown provenance; acquired.
Clay covered by a thick red slip. Bowl decorated with encircling white and black bands. On the feet black hatching. H 11·5; D 21·5.
This piece, together with others from Cyprus, was probably imported from Cilicia. The form was later imitated in the local fabrics.
Bibliography: Karageorghis, *BCH* C (1976), 841ff, fig. 5 a–b.
Cyprus Museum, Nicosia. 1975/II–17/17.

312 Chian chalice
Archaic period (600–575 BC)
Marion.
Decorated on the outside with a winged sphinx seated to the left on a ground showing geometric motifs. Black foot. Polychrome decoration in white and red on a black ground on inside showing lotus flowers and rosettes below the rim and encircling bands with a wheel in the centre. H 13·3; D 13.
Bibliography: Dikaios, *JHS* LXVI (1946), 5ff., pl. 1.a,c.
Cyprus Museum, Nicosia. 1944/1–28/2.

313 Chian bowl (phiale)
Archaic period (600–575 BC)
Marion; acquired.
Shallow dish with central boss (mesomphalos). On the exterior simple rosettes with dots below the rim and bands around the base. Rich polychrome decoration in white and red over black on the inside; in the main frieze elaborate lotuses and rosettes; the outer zone shows linked pomegranates and buds; round the omphalos, a wheel. H 4·6; D 18·5.
This and no. 312 are the two finest Chian vessels so far found at Marion. The *phiale* imitates a metal prototype and is a particularly fine clay example. Other Chian vessels recorded from Marion are wine jars and a second chalice; the

313

former have been found elsewhere in the island. These items are evidence of increasing East Greek interest in Cyprus during the sixth century.

Bibliography: Boardman, *RDAC* (1968), 12ff., pl. 4.
Cyprus Museum, Nicosia. 1952/VI–171·11.

Writing

Five different scripts are found in Iron Age Cyprus: Cypro-Syllabic, Greek, Phoenician, Cuneiform and Egyptian hieroglyphs. Most of the inscriptions are votive or funerary, except for those on coins which name the kings.

Cypro-Syllabic with its 50–60 characters, is evidently related in some way to the Cypro-Minoan script of the Late Bronze Age (nos. 144–149). It is now used to write both Greek and Eteo-Cypriote. The earliest Iron Age syllabic inscriptions that can be securely dated belong to the first half of the eighth century (as no. 314), but it was not until the seventh century that the script was in regular use, and then it lasts until the end of the third century BC. Eteo-Cypriote is still undeciphered but it appears to be a pre-Hellenic and pre-Semitic language, probably related to the native Cypriote tongue surviving from the Late Bronze Age (see also p. 53 above). The majority of Eteo-Cypriote inscriptions come from Amathus which was founded in the tenth century, probably by refugees from abandoned or destroyed Late Bronze Age centres.

The Greek alphabet appeared in the sixth century, and bilingual inscriptions such as no. 317 enabled the syllabic script to be deciphered. Phoenician inscriptions, as may be expected, are particularly common at Kition where they are found both on imported (no. 257) and locally made vessels (no. 259). It is the inscriptions that provide the best evidence for the date of arrival of the Phoenicians in Cyprus. Cuneiform and hieroglyphs are both rare but an important cuneiform document is the stele erected by Sargon II at Kition (now in Berlin) recording the submission of the Cypriote kings in 709 BC. Hieroglyphs accompany the syllabic inscriptions on the Egyptian bronze vessel from Kourion (no. 329), but it should be noted that the two inscriptions bear no relation to each other. [V.A.T.–B.]

314 Inscribed jug, White-Painted ware
Geometric/Archaic period (about 750 BC)
Region of Marion.
Decorated with a row of concentric circles. The inscription is painted on the shoulder above. Syllabic script, perhaps Eteo-Cypriote, with at least one sign related to Cypro-Minoan. H 16·5; D (greatest) 12·5.

314

This is one of the earliest Iron Age inscriptions as no. 258 from Kition.

Bibliography: Karageorghis, *AJA* LX (1956), 353, no. 4, 357, no. 2, ill.2, pl. 119.4.

Kouklia Museum. 569.

315 Inscribed jug, White-Painted ware
Archaic period (about 700 BC)
Marion; given by Archbishop Makarios.
Decorated with concentric circles with four signs on the shoulder incised after firing. Inscription probably reads *pi-lo-ti-mo*, a proper name known elsewhere in Cyprus.

The inscription appears to be contemporary with the vessel and is therefore among the earliest Iron Age syllabic inscriptions recorded.

Bibliography: Karageorghis, *BCH* LXXXVI (1962), 356, fig. 37a–b.

Cyprus Museum, Nicosia. 1961/XII–8/2.

316 Inscribed jug, Bichrome ware
Archaic period (600–500 BC)
Kornos, Tomb 1; Cyprus Archaeological Survey.

Decorated with concentric circles on the body and bands on the neck and handle. Inscription painted in black after firing. H 18·6.

Syllabic inscription in four lines with some letters missing; Greek names are decipherable in lines 3 and 4.

Bibliography: Karageorghis, *BCH* LXXXIX (1965), 294f., fig. 92; Masson, *RDAC* (1967), 168ff., fig. 1–2.

Cyprus Museum, Nicosia. CS 1375/B156.

317 Limestone funerary stele with bi-lingual inscription
Archaic period (600–500 BC)
Marion.
Greek (Ionic) inscription on the front reading κασιγνητας (of the sister); syllabic inscription with the same reading (*ka-si-ne-ta*) down the side. W 19; H 29; Th 5.

Bibliography: Mitford, *Op Ath* III (1960), 179ff., no. 1, figs. 1–2; Masson (1961), 177, no. 164, pl. 22.2–3.

Cyprus Museum, Nicosia. 1944/II–9/1.

318 Inscribed silver finger-ring
Archaic period (about 600 BC)
Unknown provenance.

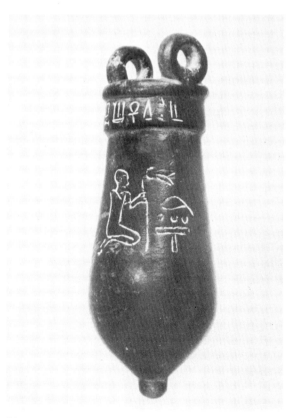

320

Cartouche ring with double bezel. Cypriote syllabic inscription mentioning? Aristagoras; a sketchily drawn bird, and a zigzag border.

Bibliography: Masson (1961), 350f., no. 367, fig. 119, pl. 61; Boardman, *Antike Kunst* (1967), 6, A2.

Cyprus Museum, Nicosia. 1934/I–15/1.

319 Inscribed silver plaque

Archaic period (600–500 BC)

Ormidhia, Lakshou tou Solomou; acquired.

Rectangular, decorated in repoussé with an animal (probably a panther) leaping to the left. Syllabic inscription naming Onasilos as dedicator. Corroded round the edges. L 4·5; W 2.

Bibliography: Masson (1961), 308, no. 307, pl. 53·2.

Cyprus Museum, Nicosia. J728.

320 Egyptian bronze situla with hieroglyph and Cypriote syllabic inscription

Archaic period (about 663–525 BC; Saite period in Egypt)

Kourion, Temple of Apollo; American excavations 1937.

The syllabic inscription reads to 'the god', who is evidently Apollo. H 11.

Bibliography: Masson (1961), 199, no. 188.

Cyprus Museum, Nicosia.

Jewellery

The jewellery of Archaic Cyprus generally follows the types of the Geometric period, but the technique is of a higher quality while the decoration is more elaborate and enriched with fine granulation. Figures are portrayed in limestone and terracotta wearing earrings, necklaces and bangles, and many of these are matched by the finds themselves. The ribbed lentoid beads from an early burial (about 775–750 BC) in a monumental tomb at Salamis (no. 217) are similar to those of the fine necklace from Arsos (no. 323) although here the ribs are shown by granulation. Identical necklaces with pendants are worn by statues of the later seventh century from the same site. The gold mountings (nos. 321, 322) continue the now familiar Syrian form decorated with oriental designs. These Cypriote pieces are contemporary with the East Greek versions from Rhodes, which adopt the form from Cyprus. The earrings likewise follow the early types, which had survived in the island through the Geometric period. [V.A.T.-B.]

321 Gold mounting

Archaic period (750–650 BC)

Paphos district.

Similar to no. 322. Rectangular with rolled edges and perforations in the corner. Pomegranate pendants attached by gold wire along the lower edge. Repoussé decoration showing a female figure in flounced skirt with her arms bent and hands held below her breasts. One pendant missing. L 6·5, (of pendant) 2·5; H 3·5.

Bibliography: Karageorghis, *BCH* XCVIII (1974), 823ff., fig. 3.

Cyprus Museum, Nicosia. 1973/IX–19/1.

322 Gold-plated silver mountings

Archaic period (700–600 BC)

Yialia, Paphos district.

Nine rectangular plaques with folded edges and perforations in the corners. All are bordered by beads of granulation and decorated in repoussé, seven showing the bust of a winged female with her hands holding her breasts and two showing lotus flowers. Some corrosion. L 2; W 2.

Compare the earlier example no. 219.

Bibliography: Pierides (1971), 26, pl. 14.2.

Cyprus Museum, Nicosia. 1945/I–23/1–1a.

321   324

Perhaps an import from the Greek trading post at Naucratis in the Egyptian Delta. A Naucratic origin would explain why such a vessel, typically Greek in shape, bears the Pharaoh's cartouche.

Bibliography: Dikaios, *JHS* LXVI (1946), 7, pl. 1d; Dikaios (1961), 154, pl. 33.16.

Cyprus Museum, Nicosia. 1941/XX–161/1.

323 Gold necklace with agate pendant
Archaic period (700–600 BC)
Arsos, sanctuary of Aphrodite; Cyprus Museum excavations 1917.
Forty lentoid beads with fine granulation. Cylindrical agate pendant decorated with lozenges and triangles in gold mountings. On top of the pendant a bee and two snakes (uraei) wearing Egyptian crowns. L 33; (of pendant) 4·5.
Bibliography: Dikaios (1961), 161f., no. 9, pl. 27.3; Pierides (1971), 27, pl. 15.
Cyprus Museum, Nicosia. J100.

324 Gold earring
Archaic period (600–475 BC)
Soloi.
Crescent-shaped and hollow. A thin wire hoop bound at the junction with the crescent by three rings on each side. Beads of granulation on two of the rings and round the edge of the crescent; pomegranate pendants hung below the crescent attached by loops. L 4.
Bibliography: Pierides (1971), 26f., pl. 14.4.
Cyprus Museum, Nicosia. J216.

325 Faience perfume bottle
Archaic period (569–525 BC)
Unknown provenance.
Decorated with the cartouche of the Egyptian Pharaoh Amasis (569–525 BC) who conquered Cyprus. H 7·3.

Bronzes

The Phoenicians who colonised part of Cyprus introduced the lamp stands supported by floral capitals (no. 326 and, in ivory, no. 225) which also reach their other favourite ports of call including Etruria, Sardinia and Carthage.

The two helmets are rare actual examples, although limestone and terracotta statues illustrate the wide variety of helmets worn in Archaic Cyprus, many of which can be paralleled on North Syrian and Assyrian reliefs of the earlier first millennium. The example from Palaepaphos (no. 327) dates from the second half of the eighth century and was imported from Urartu (in central Asia in the area of Lake Van). The Corinthian helmet (no. 328), from mainland Greece, was found in the mound built against the city wall by the Persians when besieging Palaepaphos in 498 BC. Other evidence shows that the Cypriots became acquainted with this truly Greek type during the later sixth century.

The Cypriote version of a Sicilian type of fibula (as no. 329) must be of local manufacture, like the hinged front-bands from Salamis. At present there is little direct evidence for bronze working in Cyprus in the Iron Age but it seems unlikely that the industry, so well attested in the Late Bronze Age, was not continued or revived since the island is so rich in copper. [V.A.T.-B.]

327

326 Bronze lamp stand
Archaic period (about 650–550 BC)
Unknown provenance.
Stand composed of two floral capitals with overhanging leaves. It supports arms, two of which end in volutes, joined together by a ring on which the lamp would have been placed. H 31·5.
Compare the ivory example from Salamis no. 225.
Bibliography: Karageorghis, *BCH* XCII (1968), 278, fig. 31.
Cyprus Museum, Nicosia. 1967/III–4/1.

327 Bronze helmet
Archaic period (750–650 BC)
Palaepaphos, Mavrommatis Tomb.
Conical. Repoussé decoration on the front showing a winged-sun-disc between curving lines. Perforations around lower border probably for attaching a leather lining. H 24·6; D 21·4.

328

Bibliography: Karageorghis, *BCH* XC (1966), 321f., fig. 55.
Cyprus Museum, Nicosia. 1965/XI–29/62.

328 Greek bronze helmet
Archaic period (about 500 BC)
Palaepaphos, Site A, siege mound; British excavations.
Known as the Corinthian type. L 31; H 21·5.
   Bibliography: Erdmann (1977), 25, no. 154, pl. 13.
   Cyprus Museum, Nicosia. KA 2269.

329 Bronze fibula (dress pin)
Archaic period (about 650–550 BC)
Unknown provenance; formerly Colocassides collection.
Triangular bow richly decorated with beads and discs and surmounted by a knob. Elongated catch-plate. L 10·4; H 6·75.
   Cyprus Museum, Nicosia. 1956/VI-23/1.

Sculpture

Large-scale sculpture in limestone and terracotta began in Cyprus in about 670/660 BC. The earliest, or Proto-Cypriote, style is predominantly a local, Cypriote creation, although some links with Syria can be observed. In the succeeding Neo-Cypriote style the Cypriote element was modified by Egyptian and East Greek influence. The few sculptures in the true Cypro-Egyptian style are essentially imitations of Egyptian prototypes, and must therefore belong to the period of Egyptian rule (about 569–545 BC). The earlier Egyptian influence on the Neo-Cypriote style resulted in particular from Cyprus' relations with Naucratis, the Greek trading post established in the Nile Delta. Naucratis was the home of statuettes of a 'mixed style' that was common in Rhodes, Chios and Old Smyrna in the late seventh and earlier sixth centuries. The dates and sequences of the Cypro-Greek styles are determined with reference to their Greek prototypes. Cypro-Archaic sculpture draws heavily on East Greek models and its beginning (about 540 BC) coincides with the absorption of the island into the Persian Empire. In the Sub-Archaic Cypro-Greek group of the Classical and Hellenistic periods the style becomes stagnant, but Cypro-Classical sculpture keeps close to its Greek, now Athenian, models.   [V.A.T.-B.]

330 Limestone statue of Zeus Keraunios (The Thunderer)
Archaic period (about 500 BC)
Kition sanctuary; Swedish excavations.
Bearded figure walking forward wearing a long tunic and the aegis (mantle) regularly worn by Zeus. His right arm is raised holding a thunderbolt. In his left hand he clutches the eagle. Archaic Cypro-Greek style. Thunderbolt broken and only the claws of the eagle survive, lower part of legs missing. H.56.
   Bibliography: SCE III, 32f., 57ff., nos. 139, 256, 449, pls. 14, 15·1–2.
   Cyprus Museum, Nicosia.

331 Limestone head of Athena
Archaic period (500–475 BC)
Vouni, Temple of Athena; Swedish excavations.
She wears a Corinthian helmet pushed back on her head with part of a sphinx on the top still visible. Archaic Cypro-Greek style. Partly broken. H 10·5.

Bibliography: SCE III, 101, 103, no. 210, pl. 40.
Cyprus Museum, Nicosia.

332 Limestone statue of a woman

Archaic period (510–475 BC)
Vouni palace; Swedish excavations.
She stands with her left leg slightly advanced. Her right arm, at her breasts, originally held an offering, and her left hand clutches folds of drapery. She wears a bonnet-shaped head-dress, long tunic (chiton) and cloak (himation) drawn over her left shoulder. The folds are rendered partly plastically and partly by grooves. Black and red on features and jewellery. Archaic Cypro-Greek style. Broken at the neck and below knees; left forearm missing. w (shoulder) 9·7, (waist) 5·5; H 34·7; Th (breast to back) 4·2.

Bibliography: SCE III, 231, 265f., no. 28, 40, 45, pls. 58·3, 59·1.
Cyprus Museum, Nicosia.

333 Limestone female head

Archaic period (500–475 BC)
Arsos; Cyprus Museum excavations.
She wears a low diadem decorated in relief with rosettes in pairs. Between them naked men in three-quarter view running to the right with their arms outstretched to hold the upper rosettes. Archaic Cypro-Greek style.

Bibliography: SCE III, 589, no. 79, pl. 191·4–5.
Cyprus Museum, Nicosia.

334 Limestone capital

Archaic period (about 600–500 BC)
Idalion.
Perhaps from a pilaster. A triple abacus crowns a volute capital. Low relief decoration showing volutes with a central triangle filled with a crescent and disc. Above an open palmette enclosing a frieze of lotus flowers and buds. w 106; H 89; Th 10.

Capitals of this type originated in the Near East where, used architecturally, they regularly crowned pilasters. They were copied by Cyprus but many of the Cypriote examples crown votive, free-standing monuments. The motif of this piece derived from the Near Eastern 'tree of life' is found in other media where it is often purely decorative.

Cyprus Museum, Nicosia. C 228.

330

The Classical Period

Throughout the Classical period (about 475–325 BC) Cyprus was poised between Greece and Persia. After her subjection in the Ionian revolt, the Greeks made various attempts to liberate the island from the Persians and a major expedition was launched in 450/449 BC under the Athenian commander Cimon. By now the Cypriote cities were divided in their loyalties so that the pro-Persian strongholds, including Marion, Salamis and Kition, were besieged. Marion was taken and a phil-Hellene placed on the throne, but during the siege of Kition Cimon died suddenly. By the peace of Kallias which followed in 448 BC the Athenians agreed to give up their interests in the East Mediterranean and subsequently withdrew from Cyprus leaving her once again firmly under Persian control. There was now a general anti-Hellenic movement in the island until the phil-Hellene Evagoras ascended the throne of Salamis in 411 BC. He turned again to Athens and managed to win control over most of the Cypriote cities and unite them against Persia. However, in 386 BC Athens withdrew support under the terms of the peace of Antalcidas. Left alone to face the Persians Cyprus under Evagoras was finally defeated, but a settlement was reached whereby Evagoras retained the throne of Salamis. His successors, although weaker than himself, remained phil-Hellenic and joined with Egypt and Phoenicia in another revolt against Persia in 351 BC. Nonetheless, when put to siege, possibly not until about five years later, Salamis voluntarily submitted leaving the entire forces of Cyprus at Persia's disposal.

In 336 BC Alexander the Great succeeded to the throne of Macedon and quickly secured command of Macedonia, Greece and the northern frontiers. His subsequent successes against the Persian Empire led the Cypriots to change their allegiance by 330 BC and thus put an end to Persian domination of their island for ever.

The struggles between Greece and Persia for supremacy in Cyprus had repercussions on Cypriote civilisation. Contacts were now with Achaemenid Persia and mainland Greece so that Attic rather than East Greek pottery dominated the market. The phil-Hellenic leanings of Marion after 449 BC and the

movement promoted all over Cyprus by Evagoras, led to the adoption of certain Greek forms. However, in their characteristic way the Cypriots often came to adapt rather than slavishly imitate their prototypes. They made certain versions (e.g. the spiral earrings and hair-rings, nos. 356–357, 364) their own speciality and modified others (e.g. the silver bowl, no. 347). The local pottery continued to be made in the same fabrics but the pitchers (nos. 360, 361) had figures in the Greek style on their shoulders and some were decorated with ornaments borrowed from contemporary Attic vases. The deliberate attempt by the pro-Persian group to ban all things Greek after Cimon's death led to some stagnation in style, particularly for sculpture in the round. Nonetheless some fine reliefs were carved in this period which combined Greek and oriental elements. The role of Cyprus as an intermediary continued. Certain forms like the finger-rings with relief decoration (e.g. no. 335), already popular in Cyprus in the late sixth century, now reached the Greek world and the snake bracelets (like nos. 352–354) travelled from Achaemenid Persia via Cyprus to Greece. At the end of the period, however, Cyprus of her own accord submitted to Alexander and became fully hellenised and part of the Greek world. [V. A. T.-B.]

335 Carnelian pendant
Classical period (475–400 BC)
Salamis, Cellarka cemetery, Tomb 60; Department of Antiquities excavations.
In the form of an acorn with a gold cap, decorated by engraving, with suspension loop. L 2·3.
Bibliography: Necropolis II, 99f., no. 95, pls. A.1, 145, 237. Cyprus Museum, Nicosia.

336 Gold pendant
Classical period (475–400 BC)
Salamis, Cellarka cemetery, Tomb 60; Department of Antiquities excavations.
In the form of a lidded jar with ovoid body, knobbed base and cylindrical neck pierced to hold suspension loop.
Fine granulation around neck and rim. L2.
Bibliography: Necropolis II, 99f., no. 96, pls. A.1, 145, 237. Cyprus Museum, Nicosia.

336

337 Gold pendant
Classical period (475–400 BC)
Salamis, Cellarka cemetery, Tomb 73. Department of
Antiquities excavations.
In the form of an acorn; upper part decorated by engraving;
suspension loop on top. L2.
   Bibliography: Necropolis II, 114, 116, no. 12, pls. A.1, 145,
237.
   Cyprus Museum, Nicosia.

338 Gold pendant
Classical period (475–400 BC)
Salamis, Cellarka cemetery, Tomb 73; Department of
Antiquities excavations.
In the form of a Horus eye; suspension loop on crown. H 1·2.
   Bibliography: Necropolis II, 114, 116 no. 13, pls. A.1, 153,
242.
   Cyprus Museum, Nicosia.

339 Pendant of dark green glass
Classical period (475–400 BC)
Salamis, Cellarka cemetery, Tomb 73; Department of
Antiquities excavations.
Ovoid. Pierced at the top to hold suspension loop of gold
wire. L 1·6.
   Bibliography: Necropolis II, 114, 116, no. 14, pls. A.1, 153,
242.
   Cyprus Museum, Nicosia.

340 Gold pendant
Classical period (475–400 BC)
Salamis, Cellarka cemetery, Tomb 82; Department of
Antiquities excavations.
In the form of a lidded vase. Filigree spirals on shoulder,
granulation round neck and rim; filigree four-petalled rosette
around base. H 3.
   Bibliography: Necropolis II, 122f., no. 1, pls. A.1, 157, 244.
   Cyprus Museum, Nicosia.

*341 Necklace of glass beads
Classical period (475–400 BC)
Salamis, Cellarka cemetery, Tomb 59; Department of
Antiquities excavations.
Consists of 525 circular beads. D (of beads) approx. 0·3.
   Bibliography: Necropolis II, 94, no. 36b, pl. 141
   Cyprus Museum, Nicosia.

*342 Necklace of glass beads
Classical period (475–400 BC)
Salamis, Cellarka cemetery, Tomb 59; Department of
Antiquities excavations.
Has 42 globular blue beads with a larger bead of brown glass
decorated with circular white trails in the centre. D (of beads)
approx. 0·6.
   Bibliography: Necropolis II, 94, no. 36a, pls. 141, 235.
   Cyprus Museum, Nicosia.

*343 Necklace of clay pomegranates
Classical period (475–400 BC)
Salamis, Cellarka cemetery, Pyre A; Department of Anti-
quities excavations.
Thirteen beads pierced vertically through the middle. L
(average) 2·5.
   Bibliography: Necropolis II, 170, nos. 12 etc., pl. 20.
   Cyprus Museum, Nicosia.

344 Terracotta incense burner
Classical period (475–400 BC)
Salamis, Cellarka cemetery, pyre A; Department of Anti-
quities excavations.
Tubular stem supporting shallow bowl; circular bands of
black and red around stem and bowl, black on rim; foot
blackened by fire. H 25; D (of bowl) 12.
   Bibliography: Necropolis II, 170, no. 1, pls. 16, 192.
   Cyprus Museum, Nicosia.

345 Bronze statuette of a cow
Classical period (475–400 BC)
Vouni, Temple of Athena; Swedish excavations.
Cast solid. Walking, with dowels below the hooves for at-
tachment to a plinth. L 25; H 20.

345

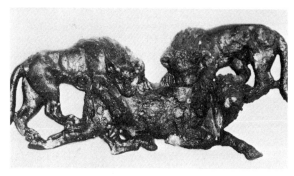

346

347

Bibliography: SCE III, 98, no. 152, pl. 44·1–2.
Cyprus Museum, Nicosia.

346 Bronze relief of a bull attacked by two lions
Classical period (475–400 BC)
Vouni, Temple of Athena; Swedish excavations.
Cast; a replica of another from the same place but not from
the same mould. L 22·5; H 9·0.
Bibliography: SCE III, 98, no. 151, pl. 42·1.
Cyprus Museum, Nicosia.

THE VOUNI TREASURE
Nos. 347–349 come from this treasure found in the palace
at Vouni. The palace was built in the early fifth century by
the then pro-Persian king of Marion, but its architecture was
altered in the mid-fifth century when a phil-Hellene ascended the throne. It was destroyed by fire in about 380 BC
and the treasure, consisting of jewellery, coins and vessels
in precious metal, was found hidden (apparently deliberately)
under a staircase leading to the upper floor.

347 Silver bowl
Classical period (450–400 BC)
Vouni palace, from the treasure; Swedish excavations.
Rounded bowl with rounded base. Tall concave rim; on the
body rosette ornaments in relief; frieze of egg-and-dart
around base of rim. D 9·6.
   A number of silver bowls of this type have been found in
Cyprus which adopts the shape from the Near East. Here
Greek influence is seen in the egg-and-dart frieze below the
rim.
Bibliography: SCE III, 238, no. 292c, pls. 90.6–7, 92.
Cyprus Museum, Nicosia.

348 Silver Cup
Classical period (450–400 BC)
Vouni palace, from the treasure; Swedish excavations.
Double curved body and moulded base; pair of horizontal
handles attached near centre of body below rim. D 12;
(between handles) 15·3.
   A typical Greek shape.
Bibliography: SCE III, 238, no. 292d, pls. 90.5, 92.
Cyprus Museum, Nicosia.

349 Pair of silver bracelets
Classical period (475–400 BC)
Vouni palace, from the treasure; Swedish excavations.
Horizontally ribbed on the outside. Engraved decoration at
each end showing an eight-petalled rosette. D 5.
Bibliography: SCE III, 238, no. 292m, pl. 89.15; Pierides
(1971), 37, pl. 25.3–4.
Cyprus Museum, Nicosia.

350 Gold necklace
Classical period (475–400 BC)
Marion.
Fifty globular ribbed beads.
   Bibliography: Karageorghis, *BCH* XC (1966), 300, fig. 6;
Pierides (1971), 33, pl. 22.1.
   Cyprus Museum, Nicosia. 1965/II–25/14.

351 Pair of gold pendants
Classical period (475–400 BC)
Marion.
In the form of vases with cylindrical necks and knobbed
bases; bead decoration around rim and neck; suspension
loop on top. H 3·5; 3.
   Bibliography: Karageorghis, *BLC* XC (1966), 300, fig. 5;
Pierides (1971), 34, pl. 22·5 (1965/II–2/16a).
   Cyprus Museum, Nicosia. 1965/II–2/16a–b.

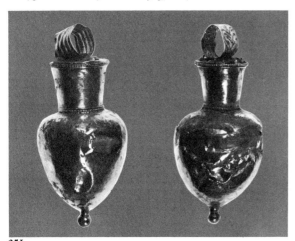

351

352 Pair of silver bracelets
Classical period (475–400 BC)
Probably from Marion.
Circular with overlapping ends terminating in snakes' heads;
details engraved. D 8·5.
   Bibliography: Karageorghis, *BCH* LXXXIX (1965), 233,
fig. 2.
   Cyprus Museum, Nicosia. 1964/1–24/9.

353 Pair of silver bracelets
Classical period (475–400 BC)
Marion.
Circular with overlapping ends terminating in snakes'
heads. Details engraved. D 6.
   Bibliography: Karageorghis, *BCH* LXXXIX (1965), 233,
fig. 3.
   Cyprus Museum, Nicosia. 1964/1–24/10.

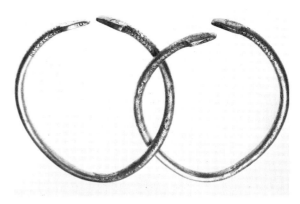

352

354 Silver bracelet
Classical period (475–400 BC)
Probably from Marion.
Made up of two half-bracelets joined together to form a
single snake bangle with overlapping ends terminating in the
heads. Engraved decoration. D 10.
   Bibliography: Karageorghis, *BCH* XCII (1968), 265, fig. 5.
   Cyprus Museum, Nicosia. 1967/III–2/1.

355 Gold finger-ring
Classical period (475–400 BC)
Marion.
Oval bezel and round flat hoop. On the bezel in relief a bee
flanked by antithetic birds. Beaded border. L (of bezel) 1·5;
D 2·5.
   Bibliography: Myres and Richter (1894), 128, no. 4154,
pl. 8; Pierides (1971), 40, pl. 27.12–13.
   Cyprus Museum, Nicosia. J376.

356 Pair of gold-plated bronze hair-rings
Classical period (475–400 BC)
Marion.
Spirals terminating in female heads with mouldings at the
other end; female heads executed in repoussé and attached
by collars with filigree ornament around the bottom. L 3·2.
   Bibliography: Karageorghis, *BCH* XC (1966), 300, fig. 4;
Pierides (1971), 29f., pl. 19.4.
   Cyprus Museum, Nicosia. 1965/II–2/9.

357 Pair of gold-plated bronze hair-rings
Classical period (475–400 BC)
Marion, Necropolis.
As no. 356, but terminating in lions' heads. L 3·2.
   Bibliography: Karageorghis, *BCH* XC (1966), 299f., fig. 3;
Pierides (1971), 30, pl. 19.5.
   Cyprus Museum, Nicosia. 1965/II–2/10.

358

358 Eight pairs of gold earrings
Classical period (475–400 BC)
Marion.
Solid hoops with overlapping ends. Terminals ribbed. D (of each earring) 1·1.
> *Bibliography:* Karageorghis, *BCH* XC (1966), 300, fig. 7.
> Cyprus Museum, Nicosia. 1965/II–2/25a–h.

359 Pair of gold earrings
Classical period (400–325 BC)
Marion.
Each is made of a rectangular gold plaque with filigree decoration bordered on either side by four gold half-globules. On the top is a round gold setting for a green glass mount. One glass setting missing. L 3·5.
> *Bibliography:* Karageorghis, *BCH* LXXXIX (1965), 235, fig. 5.
> Cyprus Museum, Nicosia. 1964/XII–4/9.

360 Pitcher, Bichrome Red ware
Classical period (475–400 BC)
Marion.
On the shoulder, a woman pouring from a miniature jug which acts as a spout. Vessel decorated on the shoulder with birds and trees below bands and chequer patterns in black; on the neck, dotted circles in black and white. Partly broken with the neck of the pouring jug missing. H 44.
> *Bibliography:* Dikaios (1961), 70, pl. 16.3.
> Cyprus Museum, Nicosia. C399.

361 Pitcher, White Painted ware
Classical period (400–325 BC)
Marion.

On the shoulder, a female figure, perhaps Psyche, pouring from a miniature pitcher which acts as a spout, accompanied by a winged Eros (a god of love); body of the vessel decorated all over with elaborate floral and geometric designs in zones. Partly broken, neck of small pitcher missing. H 40·5; D (greatest) 22·5.
> *Bibliography:* Dikaios (1961), 68, pl. 16.4.
> Cyprus Museum, Nicosia.

362 Limestone grave relief
Classical period (about 450 BC)
Marion.
In high relief within a niche a woman dressed in a long tunic and a cap. Crowned by a finial decorated in low relief with palmette and S-shaped spirals. Short projection below for insertion into base. Traces of red paint. W 21·8; H 55·5; Th 11·5.
This attractive monument combines a Greek ornament similar to that crowning gravestones shown on contemporary or slightly earlier Attic vases (white-ground lekythoi) with the typical Cypriote motif of a frontal figure in high relief.
> Cyprus Museum, Nicosia. 1948/V–12/1.

363 Gold finger-ring
Classical period (475–400 BC)
Unknown provenance.
Swivel ring with onyx stone in a plain setting. Rounded solid hoop. On the bezel a bull running to the left. L (of bezel) 2; D 3.
> *Bibliography:* Pierides (1971), 38, pl. 26.9.
> Cyprus Museum, Nicosia. 1955/III–8/1.

364 Pair of silver hair-rings
Classical period (475–400 BC)
Limassol, Kapsalos necropolis.
Similar to nos. 356, 357, but the collar is decorated on the front with a six-petalled rosette inlaid with enamel of light green and dark blue. L 4.
> *Bibliography:* Karageorghis, *BCH* LXXXVIII (1964), 326, fig. 58.
> Limassol Museum. 337/61.

365 Pair of gold earrings
Classical period (400–325 BC)
Soloi, tomb; Cyprus Archaeological Survey.
Plain hoops terminating in lions' heads; fine filigree decoration. D 1.
> *Bibliography:* Karageorghis, *BCH* XCII (1968), 284f., fig. 53; Pierides (1971), 32, pl. 21.4–5.
> Cyprus Museum, Nicosia. CS 1661/2a,b.

366 Pair of gold earrings
Classical period (400–375 BC)
Soloi; Cyprus Archaeological Survey.
Plain hoops terminating in horned lions' heads; fine filigree
decoration.
  Bibliography: Karageorghis, *BCH* XCII (1968), 284,
fig. 51.
  Cyprus Museum, Nicosia. CS 1668/6.

367 Pair of gold earrings
Classical period (400–325 BC)
Kalon Chorion, Nicosia district.
Circular hoops of twisted wire each terminating in a winged
sphinx seated on a rectangular base decorated with filigree
and granulation. On their heads, red stones in gold settings.
H (of sphinxes) 3; D 3·5.
  Bibliography: Pierides (1971), 31, pl. 20.10–11.
  Cyprus Museum, Nicosia. J260.

368, 369 Two terracotta bulls
Classical period (475–400 BC)
Potamos tou Kambou, sanctuary; Cyprus Archaeological
Survey.
Moulded, with horns and a hump on the neck. L 21·3; H 17·7.
  Bibliography: Karageorghis, *BCH* XCIV (1970), 211,
fig. 47a–b.
  Cyprus Museum, Nicosia. CS 1728/194, 204.

370 Terracotta incense burner
Classical period (465–400 BC)
Potamos tou Kambou, sanctuary (with nos. 368, 369);
Cyprus Archaeological Survey.
Tubular stem supporting a shallow bowl with out-turned rim
covered by a conical lid with a series of perforations around
the top. H 75; D (of bowl) 18.
  Bibliography: Karageorghis, *BCH* XCIV (1970), 211,
fig. 46.
  Cyprus Museum, Nicosia. CS 1728/197, 202, 203.

Select Glossary

Ajouré *see* Openwork

Amphora A large vessel used for storing wine; undecorated (or coarse ware) examples were used for transporting wine.

Andesite An acidic volcanic rock.

Askos A flask for pouring

Astarte The mother and fertility goddess worshipped throughout the Phoenician world.

Athena Daughter of Zeus, patron goddess of Athens, widely worshipped in the Greek world.

Baal Literally 'lord' but used on its own as the name of a Phoenician god or combined with another name (e.g. Baal-Melqart).

Base Ring ware Hand-made. A monochrome fabric fired brown in different shades often with a black core. Covered by a red, brown or black slip usually burnished. Often decorated with relief lines and sometimes decorated with matt white paint. The name was chosen since many vessels in this fabric have a distinct ring base, but there are exceptions.

'Bes' An Egyptian dwarf god, one of whose attributes was to dispel evil.

Bichrome ware Wheel-made. Buff or greenish-white surface with the ornaments painted in matt black and red or purplish-red.

Bichrome Red ware Wheel-made. Clay and slip as Black-on-Red ware, but the ornaments are painted in black and white or, occasionally, red.

Black-on-Red ware Wheel-made. Reddish brown clay covered by a red or reddish brown slip on which the ornaments are painted in matt black.

Black Polished ware *see* Red Polished ware

Burnished Polished. A pebble or large tooth was often used for burnishing pottery.

Centaur. A legendary monster with the torso of a human and the body of a horse.

Chalcolithic period Literally the copper-stone age which in Cyprus refers to the years between the Neolithic and Early Bronze Age.

Cloison, Cloisonné A cloison is a cell formed by thin strips of metal soldered to a background. Cloisonné is inlay work when the cells are filled with another substance such as enamel.

Combed ware Hand-made. The surface is covered with a thick red slip (coating) decorated by drawing a comb-like instrument over the surface while still wet.

Embossing, Embossed *see* Repoussé

Engraving Patterns produced by cutting into a surface with a sharp tool.

Faience Glazed powdered quartz.

Filigree A pattern of wires for decoration usually soldered to a background.

Glossy Burnished ware Hand-made. Covered with a lustrous slip and burnished.

Granulation Decoration comprising small grains or balls of metal soldered to a background.

Grey Polished ware Wheel-made. Grey clay covered with a grey polished slip.

Horus An Egyptian god, whose eye, on its own, was used as a talisman.

Kernos A ring-shaped vessel, often with plastic ornaments, normally for ritual use.

Krater A vessel for mixing wine with water.

Melqart The chief god of the Phoenician city of Tyre who became the principal god of the Phoenicians in general. Originally a solar deity, he came to have marine attributes as well. The Greeks equated him with Heracles.

Mycenaean ware The vases are wheel-made and both vessels and figurines are technically of a high standard. The clay is usually buff or light orange covered by a slip of the same or slightly lighter colour with the ornaments applied in lustrous or matt paint varying from black or dark-brown to bright red.

Niello A black composition of metallic alloys.

Obsidian Natural volcanic glass, usually black.

Openwork (Ajouré) An open pattern of any type, as one formed by cutting holes through pieces of sheet-metal.

Red and Black Burnished ware Hand-made. Monochrome pottery whose colour is determined by the firing conditions; finally the vessel was burnished.

Red-on-White ware Hand-made. The surface sometimes covered by a thin buff slip or simply smoothed and the pattern drawn in red on the white ground.

Red Polished ware Hand-made. Prevalent for a remarkably long time, the dominant ware for almost 800 years. Although clays used in the process of manufacture might vary, the sequence remained unchanged: prior to firing a thick solution of red or brown clay was applied to the surface of the vessel or figurine; it was then burnished both for appearance sake and to make the walls less porous. In the course of firing certain areas of the entire vessel or figurine might be intentionally blackened (the latter then becomes Black Polished ware). Early Bronze Age pottery is characterised by modelled ornament and incised motifs which become more intricate in the second millennium. A filling of white lime in the incisions helped to emphasise the designs.

Red Slip ware Wheel-made. Reddish-brown clay covered by a red or reddish-brown slip.

Repoussé (Embossing) Relief ornamentation produced on sheet-metal with a hammer or punches applied from behind.

Rhyton A horn-shaped drinking vessel.

Slip A thin solution of clay applied as a coating over the body of a vessel or figurine before firing.

Stamping Similar to repoussé but the ends of the punches are shaped to the desired pattern, which can then be reproduced.

Steatite Commonly known as soapstone, usually grey or greyish-green.

White Painted ware (Bronze Age) Usually hand-made with a slip in beige or another colour (such as white, yellow or grey). Painted decoration most often in black or chocolate brown.

White Painted ware (after about 1125 BC) Wheel-made. Buff or greenish-white surface on which the ornaments are painted in matt black or brown.

Abbreviations and Select Bibliography

AA: Archäologischer Anzeiger. Berlin.

AfO: Archiv für Orientforschung. Berlin.

AJA: American Journal of Archaeology. New York.

Arch. Rep.: Archaeological Reports. London (published with *Journal of Hellenic Studies*).

BCH: Bulletin de correspondence héllenique. Athens.

Benson (1973): J. L. Benson, *The Necropolis of Kaloriziki. Studies in Mediterranean Archaeology* XXXVI. Göteborg, 1973.

BSA: Annual of the British School at Athens. London.

Buchholz and Karageorghis (1973): H. G. Buchholz and V. Karageorghis, *Prehistoric Greece and Cyprus.* London, 1973.

Catling (1964): H. W. Catling, *Cypriot bronzework in the Mycenaean world.* Oxford, 1964.

Dikaios (1940): P. Dikaios, 'The excavations at Vounous— Bellapais in Cyprus, 1931–2, *Archaeologia* LXXXVIII (1940), 1ff.

Dikaios (1953): P. Dikaios, *Khirokitia*, Oxford, 1953.

Dikaios (1961): P. Dikaios, *Guide to the Cyprus Museum.* 3rd ed. Nicosia, 1961.

Enkomi: P. Dikaios, *Enkomi*, I–III. Mainz, 1969, 1971.

Erdmann (1977): E. Erdmann, *Ausgrabungen in Alt-Paphos auf Cypern*, I. Konstanz, 1977.

Gjerstad (1926): E. Gjerstad, *Studies on Prehistoric Cyprus.* Stockholm, 1920.

Higgins (1961): R. A. Higgins, *Greek and Roman Jewellery.* London, 1961.

JHS: Journal of Hellenic Studies. London.

Karageorghis (1962): V. Karageorghis, *Treasures in the Cyprus Museum.* Nicosia, 1962.

Karageorghis (1965): V. Karageorghis, *Nouveaux documents pour l'étude du bronze récent à Chypre.* Paris, 1965.

Karageorghis and des Gagniers (1974): V. Karageorghis and J. des Gagniers, *La céramique chypriote de style figuré.* Rome, 1974.

Karageorghis (1975): V. Karageorghis, *Alaas. A Protogeometric necropolis in Cyprus.* Nicosia, 1975.

Karageorghis (1976): V. Karageorghis, *Kition. Mycenaean and Phoenician Discoveries in Cyprus.* London, 1976.

Karageorghis (1977): V. Karageorghis, *Two Cypriote sanctuaries of the end of the Cypro-Archaic Period.* Nicosia, 1977.

Karageorghis (1977): J. Karageorghis, *La Grande Déesse de Chypre et son Culte.* Lyon, 1977.

Kition: V. Karageorghis, *et al., Excavations at Kition/ Fouilles de Kition*, I–III. Nicosia, 1974–77.

Masson (1961): O. Masson, *Les Inscriptions Chypriotes Syllabiques.* Paris, 1961.

Myres and Richter (1899): J. L. Myres and M. Ohnefalsch-Richter, *A Catalogue of the Cyprus Museum.* Oxford, 1899.

Necropolis: V. Karageorghis, *Excavations in the Necropolis of Salamis*, I–IV. Nicosia, 1967–78.

Op. Ath.: Opuscula Atheniensia. Lund.

Pierides (1971): A. Pierides, *Jewellery in the Cyprus Museum.* Nicosia, 1971.

RDAC: Report of the Department of Antiquities of Cyprus. Nicosia.

SCE: E. Gjerstad, *et al., The Swedish Cyprus Expedition.* Stockholm/Lund, 1934–72.

Schaeffer (1936): C. F. A. Schaeffer, *Missions en Chypre 1932–5.* Paris, 1936.

Schaeffer (1952): C. F. A. Schaeffer, *Enkomi—Alasia*, I. Paris, 1952.

Stewart (1950): E. and J. Stewart, *Vounous 1937–8.* Lund, 1950.

Strong (1966): D. E. Strong, *Greek and Roman gold and silver plate.* London, 1966.

Young (1955): J. H. and S. H. Young, *Terracotta figurines from Kourion in Cyprus.* Philadelphia, 1955.

Index of Sites

(References are to catalogue numbers)